Herman Melville's
MOBY-DICK

Lawrence MacPhee

Assistant Professor of English
Seton Hall University

This edition published by Barnes & Noble, Inc.,
by arrangement with Macmillan Publishing USA,
a division of Simon & Schuster, Inc.

1998 Barnes & Noble Books

MACMILLAN is a registered trademark of Macmillan, Inc.
Monarch and colophons are trademarks of Simon & Schuster, Inc.,
registered in the U.S. Patent and Trademark Office.

Macmillan Publishing USA
A division of Simon & Schuster, Inc.
1633 Broadway
New York, NY 10019

ISBN 0-7607-0645-X

Text design by Tony Meisel

Printed and bound in the United States of America.

98 99 00 01 02 03 M 9 8 7 6 5 4 3 2 1

RRDC

CONTENTS

BIOGRAPHICAL NOTE ON HERMAN MELVILLE

Born into a family of substantial means in New York City on August 19, 1819, Herman Melville spent a secure and comfortable childhood. His maternal grandfather, Peter Gansevoort, had served as a general in the American Revolution, and his father, Allan Melvill (his father's spelling for the family name) was a successful importer. In 1830, however, Melvill suffered heavy financial losses, followed by a serious illness which ended in his death in 1832.

Shocked by the death of the father whom he idolized, Melville moved with his family to Albany, where he attended the Albany Classical School. His restless nature and constant conflicts with his mother soon brought an end to his formal education. However, he was an avid reader of the books from his father's library. Melville soon drifted into a variety of occupations. He worked for a time as a clerk for an older brother, as a messenger for a bank, and later, as a country schoolteacher near his uncle's home in Pittsfield, Massachusetts. In 1839, he signed on a British merchant ship, the St. Lawrence, bound to Liverpool and back, a trip which provided the material for his novel, *Redburn* (1849), and the impetus for an extended period of travel and adventure. Although he again tried teaching school on his return from Liverpool, he soon resigned, joining the whaler Acushnet as an ordinary seaman in 1841.

Melville suffered the hardship of life aboard a mid-nineteenth century whaler until he could no longer tolerate it. Accordingly, he and a shipmate Tobias Greene (who appears as Toby in *Typee*) deserted the ship at Nukuheva in the Marquesas Islands. Here Melville spent a month as the captive of a cannibal tribe, and finally escaped aboard the Australian whaler the Lucy Ann, which he left a short time later at Tahiti. Again after a short stay working at a variety of occupations, he signed aboard the whaler Charles and Henry, and arrived in Hawaii in April, 1843. Here, after working for a short time as a warehouse clerk, he joined the U.S. Navy and was assigned to the frigate United States. After visits to Mexico and South America, he was discharged in New York City in October, 1844, and with the exception of a few trips later in his life, he closed forever the period of his adventures.

In the years immediately following his travels, Melville began his career as a writer. In 1846 he published *Typee,* a somewhat exaggerated and imaginative account of his stay among the Typee islanders, and in 1847 its sequel, *Omoo.* These were followed by *Mardi* (1849), an allegorical novel quite different from its predecessors and the precursor of Moby Dick. Attempting to atone for the failure of *Mardi,* Melville returned to the method of his earlier adventure books with *Redburn* (1849), which borrowed material from his first voyage to Liverpool in 1839; and *White Jacket* (1850), which enlarged upon his experience as a seaman aboard the United States.

Although his first five books had won him considerable fame and some financial security, Melville still felt dissatisfied with his work, and in 1851 he published *Moby-Dick,* which although a failure in its day, has since become his best-known work. It was also during these first few years at home that Melville became established as an important member of the New York literary scene. He formed a friendship with Nathaniel Hawthorne, who encouraged and supported Melville throughout the writing of *Moby-Dick.* Melville dedicated the book to him with the following inscription: "In token of my admiration for his genius, this book is inscribed to Nathaniel Hawthorne."

In 1847, Melville married Elizabeth Shaw, the daughter of the Chief Justice of Massachusetts, and in the fall of that year moved from Pittsfield, Massachusetts to New York City. Early in 1850, after a brief trip to London to make arrangements for the publication of *White Jacket,* the Melvilles moved to "Arrowhead," a farm in Pittsfield, Massachusetts where they remained for the next thirteen years.

The critical reaction to *Moby-Dick* was negative. Melville's next novel, *Pierre* (1852), which attacked conventional morality and publishing practices, had an even worse reception by the critics as well as the book-buying public. Angry, disappointed, and suffering ill health, Melville turned for a time to writing articles and short stories for *Putnam's* and *Harper's* magazines. Among his works of this period are *Israel Potter* (1855), which had been first published serially, and *Piazza Tales* (1856), a collection of short stories which included "Bartelby the Scrivener" and "Benito Cereno." In 1857, he published his last novel, *The Confidence Man,* a satiric tale that has its setting on a Mississippi River steamboat, and like *Moby-Dick* has since aroused much critical interest.

His career now at its lowest ebb, Melville traveled through the Mediterranean countries and the Holy Land on borrowed money, and on his return attempted to make a living lecturing on such subjects as "statuary in Rome" and "the South Seas." Unsuccessful, he sold his farm at Pittsfield, paid his debts with the remaining money, and bought a house in New York City where he secured a job in the Custom House. He held this job until he retired in 1885.

During these years and those that followed, Melville published several volumes of poetry, including: *Battle Pieces and Aspects of the War* (1866), *Clarel: a Poem and a Pilgrimage in the Holy Land* (1876), *John Marr and Other Sailors* (1888), and *Timoleon* (1891). These last three volumes were for the most part privately printed in small editions at the expense of an uncle, Peter Gansevoort.

At his death on September 28, 1891, Melville left in manuscript a considerable number of verses as well as the short novel, *Billy Budd,* which was not published until 1924. It achieved much critical acclaim, inspired an opera by the great English composer Benjamin Britten, and accelerated an already reviving interest in Melville.

MOBY-DICK
CHAPTERS 1–9

CHAPTER 1: LOOMINGS

Ishmael tells us that "some years ago—never mind how long precisely" he decided to go to sea to drive away a feeling of melancholy and moodiness. This is his way of forgetting the difficulties of life on shore. Let other men commit suicide if they can't face their troubles, but Ishmael will go to sea when, as he puts it, he finds himself "involuntarily pausing before coffin warehouses, and bringing up the rear of every funeral I meet."

There is nothing unusual about the urge to sail the ocean, Ishmael assures us. Look at the wharves of Manhattan on Sunday afternoon, and you will see thousands of men staring out to sea. If we leave Manhattan and go to the country, we still find that water mysteriously attracts men. A country path, in a region of lakes, leads to a pool or stream. The artist painting a landscape includes a stream in his picture. The visitor to the prairies is disappointed because there is no water there. In ancient times, the Greeks and Persians regarded the seas with reverence. In other words, at all times and in all places, the sea has exercised a strange fascination for the human race.

When Ishmael goes to sea, he chooses to ship as a common sailor, because he gets paid for his work and because the work he does is healthy and fairly active. True enough, he may be ordered around by a dictatorial officer, but both in life and on board, everyone is under the command of someone else. (Ishmael says, "Who ain't a slave? Tell me that.") Even the commander of the ship is not as free as he thinks he is. His air comes to him second-hand; the lowly sailors, stationed toward the bow of the ship, breathe it first.

Ishmael tells us that he chose a whaling ship for this voyage, but he cannot explain why. The Fates, he supposes, must have had a hand in his decision. Nonetheless, he admits, he was dazzled by the idea of the whale itself—and had a powerful desire to see the marvelous creature in some remote corner of the world.

COMMENT

In the Bible, Ishmael is the son of Abraham and a slave woman, Hagar. Sarah, Abraham's wife, insisted that he abandon Hagar and Ishmael, and Ishmael became an outcast. The name is symbolic of the wanderer or displaced person. Since the Ishmael in the novel introduces himself with the words "Call me Ishmael," it is evidently not his real name.

Ishmael suspects that free will may not exist at all. "Ain't we all slaves?" is his comment on life in general, as well as life aboard ship, and his insistence on the role of "those stage managers, the Fates" implies that he thinks man's life may be determined by forces beyond his control.

CHAPTER 2: THE CARPET-BAG

Taking his carpet-bag, Ishmael leaves Manhattan for New Bedford, Massachusetts. He plans to take a ship sailing from Nantucket Island. He feels that it would be unfitting to sail from any other port, for Nantucket is the original home of whaling in America. Arriving at New Bedford, Ishmael discovers that he has missed the packet boat to the island, and must spend two nights and a day in New Bedford. He therefore looks for an inn for the night, but cannot find anything appropriate to his finances and his mood. He sees The Crossed Harpoons and The Swordfish, but both look "too jolly and expensive." Finally, he comes upon an inn whose sign reads "The Spouter-Inn: Peter Coffin." He decides to stay here, although he has misgivings about the ominous name of the landlord.

CHAPTER 3: THE SPOUTER-INN

Ishmael enters the Spouter-Inn, and finds that it is so low and dark that it reminds him of the interior of a condemned ship. An extraordinary painting on one side of the entry catches his attention. It is so shadowy and grimy that he cannot discern its subject. Eventually, he decides that it shows a gigantic whale about to plunge bodily onto the masts and deck of a foundering ship. On the opposite wall Ishmael sees a collection of clubs, spears, and tools used in the whaling industry, many of them made of the bones and teeth of the whale itself. These ugly weapons cause Ishmael to shudder because of their appearance and their bloody functions. At the back of the inn is the bar, which is entered through an archway made of the jawbone of a whale.

COMMENT

Melville has given the story a somewhat disturbing turn. Not only is the inn called the "Spouter" (a spouter is, of course, a whale), but one of its doorways is a whale's jaw, the bartender is called Jonah, there are whale's teeth and bones everywhere, and a picture suggesting the terrifying destructiveness of the whale is immediately evident. To enter the Spouter-Inn is, in other words, very much like entering the belly of the whale, as Jonah did in the Bible. Melville is warning the reader that the whale and the sea will swallow up men as the story develops.

Ishmael asks Peter Coffin for a bed, and is told that he will have to share one with a harpooner. Uneasily he accepts the proprietor's terms, and awaits the arrival of his unwelcome roommate. Meanwhile the crew of a newly returned whaling ship burst into the inn, and the men drink and celebrate loudly. One man, a magnificent giant named Bulkington, quietly slips out of the inn and disappears.

Increasingly ill at ease because the harpooner has not yet

appeared, Ishmael questions Peter Coffin further and finds that his bed mate is a native of the South Pacific who is in New Bedford trying to sell his collection of human heads. Apprehensive at this news, Ishmael decides to go to bed quickly and hope that all will be well. Before he can get to sleep, however, his roommate enters, and Ishmael watches in fascination as the man prepares for bed. He is tattooed from head to foot with grotesque figures, he wears a stovepipe hat, and he smokes a pipe that also functions as a tomahawk. Startled to find a stranger in his bed, the harpooner threatens to brain Ishmael with the tomahawk. Ishmael shouts for help, and a grinning Peter Coffin rushes in to introduce him to Queequeg, his bunkmate. After explanations have been made, both men are satisfied, and they settle down to sleep.

COMMENT

This chapter gives the first hints of the real terrors of whaling. Besides the omens already mentioned, remember the hideous sickle-shaped spear which Ishmael describes in this chapter—Moby Dick's deformed jaw is described as a sickle more than once in the novel.

Note Ishmael's reaction to Queequeg. Although he panics at Queequeg's exotic appearance, he quickly recognizes his friendliness and kindness. He attempts to judge Queequeg by his manner, not by his appearance.

Note that this chapter, serious though it is, contains several gleams of a rather sardonic humor; Ishmael's first encounter with Queequeg is shot full of comic horror.

CHAPTER 4: THE COUNTERPANE

Ishmael awakens the next morning to find Queequeg's arm thrown over him. He notices that Queequeg's tattooed arm and the counterpane (quilt) blend with each other, so that he can hardly distinguish Queequeg's arm except by its weight. He then recalls a peculiar experience from his childhood, in which, having been sent to bed supperless on the longest day of the year, he awoke in the middle of the night feeling that a supernatural hand had been placed in his own. He has never been able to explain this phenomenon to himself. Shocked back to reality by the realization that he has just rolled over on Queequeg's tomahawk, Ishmael begins to push and shout at his companion. Queequeg awakens, sits up stiffly, and then leaps out of bed to dress. To Ishmael's astonishment, he first puts on his hat, then crawls under the bed, seeking a private place to put on his boots. After scrambling out again, Queequeg finishes dressing and proceeds to shave with the head of his harpoon.

COMMENT

Queequeg's hugging Ishmael in a "matrimonial sort of style" foreshadows the strong friendship which the two men will share. Queequeg's habits serve not only to make him a striking and memorable character, but also show us the breadth of Ishmael's warm and humorous sympathy. The fact that Queequeg shaves with the blade of his harpoon suggests how the incidentals of whaling subtly permeate the whaleman's life and give it a special atmosphere.

CHAPTER 5: BREAKFAST

Ishmael follows Queequeg downstairs to the breakfast table, and notices Peter Coffin grinning at him. He bears Coffin no grudge for his little joke, because there are too few laughs in the world and he is glad to have been the source of another's harmless enjoyment. As he looks around the table, he notices that he can tell how long a man has been ashore by the degree to which his tan has faded. To his surprise, these brave and hardy men are shy and ill at ease with one another. Queequeg alone shows none of this shyness; he reaches the length of the table and spears pieces of beefsteak with the ever-present harpoon. After breakfast, Queequeg smokes his pipe while Ishmael goes out for a stroll.

COMMENT

Ishmael continues to show himself a close observer of men and their behavior. He is beginning to admire Queequeg, especially for his calm self-possession under all circumstances. In the whaleboats, the harpooneer is the all-important figure, and Queequeg's self-assurance shows that he is aware of this relatively exalted position. It also suggests his fearlessness, which he will demonstrate on many occasions.

CHAPTER 6: THE STREET

Strolling about the streets of New Bedford, Ishmael realizes that Queequeg is by no means the oddest spectacle to be seen in the whaling industry. He is no more outlandish than the back-country dandy who decides to go to sea. Ishmael comments wryly on the fancy clothing worn by the Green Mountain bumpkin—clothing that will collapse in a moment under the furious strain of working in a tempest at sea. But New Bedford has its beauties, too—fine parks, streets, mansions, and blooming young women. None of these would exist in New Bedford, Ishmael implies, if it had not been for the whaling industry.

CHAPTER 7: THE CHAPEL

After returning from his stroll, Ishmael decides to go out again to pay a visit to a special whaleman's chapel in New Bedford. A driving, sleety storm has replaced the fine clear weather of the morning, and the walk to the chapel is difficult and unpleasant. Shaking the sleet from his coat and hat, Ishmael looks around the chapel and notes the austere marble tablets commemorating those who died battling whales. He also notices that the mourners sit apart from one another, deliberately isolated, "as if each silent grief were insular and incommunicable." He is surprised to see Queequeg among those present, especially since Queequeg cannot read the inscriptions in the chapel.

Ishmael sympathizes with the mourners present, for they haven't even the consolation of a grave to visit; their dead lie shrouded in unknown waters thousands of miles away. As he contemplates such a burial, Ishmael reflects that the fate of the whalemen named on those frigid tablets may well be his own, and is temporarily depressed. His spirits rise again, however, for only his body can be killed by a whale—as he concludes, "stave (kill) my soul, Jove himself cannot."

COMMENT

For the second time, Ishmael has come from brutally cold weather into a building that contains unsettling references to the whale. Melville may be suggesting through Ishmael's experiences that the choices facing men are all unpleasant and dangerous. Be that as it may, Ishmael asserts his absolute independence: Whether a man is free or not, even the Fates cannot destroy his individuality—a man can preserve his integrity regardless of circumstances.

CHAPTER 8: THE PULPIT

Shortly after Ishmael takes a seat, a robust old man enters the chapel and advances to the pulpit. This is the chaplain, Father Mapple, a man who was a whaleman and harpooner as a youth, but who has devoted himself to the ministry for many years. Father Mapple's entrance calls Ishmael's attention to the pulpit, which is an extraordinary structure, so high that it reminds Ishmael of the bow of a ship. When Father Mapple starts to ascend to the pulpit by way of a ship's ladder, Ishmael fears momentarily that the chaplain may be a mere performer rather than a sincere preacher, but he concludes that the peculiarity of Mapple's method "must symbolize something unseen." Perhaps, thinks Ishmael, the isolation Mapple achieves in the pulpit severs him from worldly considerations for the moment, making him fitter to lead spiritually. While musing on this matter, Ishmael notices an odd painting on the wall behind the pulpit: it represents a ship sailing against a terrible storm, and shows the face of an angel beaming down on the scene, throwing a spot of light upon the ship's deck. Ishmael reflects that "the storm of God's quick wrath" is first seen from the pulpit, and that "the world's a ship on its passage out, and not a voyage complete; and the pulpit is its prow."

CHAPTER 9: THE SERMON

As Ishmael watches, Father Mapple gives brisk directions to his scattered congregation: "Starboard gangway . . . to larboard—larboard gangway to starboard! Midships! Midships!" The worshippers all move to the center of the chapel, and Mapple begins his sermon. First he says a brief prayer, and then leads his congregation in a hymn expressing Jonah's fears in the belly of the whale that swallowed him. The hymn ends on the note of joy Jonah felt when he was delivered from the whale. Mapple then proceeds into a powerful discourse on Jonah's attempt to flee from God, stressing that Jonah's sin "was in his willful disobedience of the command of God . . . which he found a hard command." Mapple warns that all God's commands are difficult, and that we must disobey ourselves—a difficult task—if we are to obey God.

COMMENT

Father Mapple's insistence that the group in the chapel gather together suggests the need of unity among men if any worthy end is to be achieved. The hymn that is sung stresses conflict between man and whale. Ishmael mentions that the hymn drowns out the storm, suggesting that faith can triumph over the forces that buffet men about the world.

Mapple retells the Biblical story of Jonah as a contemporary whaling story. With such sentences as "How plainly [Jonah]'s a fugitive! no baggage, not a hat-box, valise, or carpet-bag— no friends accompany him to the wharf with their adieux" and "Harry, lad, I guess he's the adulterer that broke jail in old Gomorrah," Mapple translates the story into modern terms with which his congregation strongly identifies. Jonah, who has killed his father, tries to escape God's wrath by sailing across the world. The ship sails, runs into a tremendous storm and seems about to founder. The mariners blame this bad luck on Jonah, and throw him overboard. A whale swallows Jonah, and the sea calms. In the whale's belly, Jonah repents, prays for deliverance, and is saved after three days. Mapple concludes his sermon by drawing a moral from Jonah's adventure: "Man must obey God, in spite of any difficulties, and leaders among me, such as captains and priests, must be even more responsible."

COMMENT

This is one of the most important and most dramatic chapters in the book. The story of Jonah foreshadows Ahab's basic course of action throughout the book. Ahab will not disobey himself to obey God. He will sail to the ends of the earth on what seems to be an ungodly mission. He will skulk below decks, like Jonah, at the start of the voyage. He will, like Jonah, see a distorted world by the swinging lamp in his cabin, especially as he reads his charts (Chapter 44). (Jonah's swinging lamp is the first of a great many important light, fire, and lightning images in the novel.) He will have a crucial encounter with a whale.

Father Mapple's colloquial retelling of the story of Jonah makes a strikingly original sermon. Mapple's style helps to involve his congregation, because he speaks in terms that relate to their everyday lives. Mapple makes the story of Jonah a contemporary yarn, rather than a historical anecdote of centuries past that has nothing to do with life in nineteenth-century New Bedford.

MOBY-DICK
CHAPTERS 10–29

CHAPTER 10: A BOSOM FRIEND

Returning to the Spouter-Inn, Ishmael finds Queequeg silently whittling at the nose of his little wooden idol. He watches Queequeg carefully, and concludes that there is something naturally admirable about him. "You cannot hide the soul," says Ishmael, and Queequeg seems to have a noble soul. He is twenty thousand miles from home, yet he preserves his own dignity and individuality, completely self-sufficient in an alien culture. Ishmael's heart goes out to this solitary savage, and he strikes up a conversation with him. They look through a book together, and Queequeg is taken by Ishmael's friendliness. The two smoke a pipe together, whereupon Queequeg presses his forehead against Ishmael's and announces that they are "married," that is, that they are now lifelong friends. He gives Ishmael several gifts, and then divides his money and gives half to Ishmael. The two go to their room, where Queequeg offers his evening worship, asking Ishmael to join him. Ishmael, feeling that since his duty as a Christian is to want Queequeg to worship with him, feels it is only appropriate that he reciprocate. After they make an offering to the idol and bow to it, the two retire to bed, "a cosy, loving pair."

COMMENT

Again, Ishmael displays his common sense and open mind. He sees past Queequeg's exotic tattoos to his kind heart and noble soul, and he feels it is perfectly appropriate that they worship Queequeg's idol together, just as Queequeg attended Father Mapple's sermon. The friendship is obviously based on the genuine liking, which is possible when there is no prejudice on either side.

CHAPTER 11: NIGHTGOWN

Ishmael and Queequeg nap and chat in bed for some time, but become restless in the middle of the night. Once again the two men light up Queequeg's tomahawk pipe, and, sitting up in bed, Queequeg begins to tell Ishmael his life story.

CHAPTER 12: BIOGRAPHICAL

Queequeg tells Ishmael that he comes from Kokovoko, an island in the South Pacific. His father was a great chief, a king. As a young man, Queequeg won passage to the western and Christian world by his persistence—he boarded a ship and seized a ringbolt on the deck, refusing to let go under any circumstances. Ishmael asks Queequeg if he plans to return to his island home, and Queequeg responds that he feels he has been too much exposed to Christians to be a pure enough pagan to rule over his people. He hopes to return home when he feels himself baptized again. He adds that his immediate plan is to go to sea on a whaler, and the two men decide to ship together and share their luck.

COMMENT

Queequeg's comments about the Christians among whom he has spent much of his life are interesting. He is aware of hypocrisy among Christians, having seen that many are "miserable and wicked," and has decided to die a pagan. Melville's idea that a pagan point of view is just as valid as a Christian one, and that Christianity is open to criticism, was a radical attitude in the United States in the nineteenth century.

CHAPTER 13: WHEELBARROW

The following morning, Ishmael and Queequeg settle their account with Peter Coffin and prepare to sail to Nantucket. They rent a wheelbarrow to cart their belongings to the Nantucket schooner, and while walking to the dock Queequeg tells Ishmael that when he first used a wheelbarrow, he had carried both the barrow and its contents on his head! When Ishmael laughs at this absurdity, Queequeg tells him of a ship's captain's ridiculous breach of propriety at a South Pacific wedding feast. All parts of the world have usages that are likely to seem odd or laughable to strangers.

COMMENT

Queequeg's stories, suggesting the relativity of values, extend the theme that a variety of viewpoints and values are valid.

The two men board the schooner, which sails briskly out of New Bedford. A stupid passenger makes fun of Queequeg's exotic appearance, and Queequeg, without visible anger, throws the bumpkin up into the air, causing him to turn a somersault and land on the deck on his feet. Just as the captain arrives to scold Queequeg, a boom on the ship's mast breaks loose, knocking the oafish passenger overboard and threatening to capsize the little ship. Queequeg lassoes the terrifying boom, which looks like "the lower jaw of an exasperated whale," and then leaps overboard to save the buffoon from drowning in the icy waters. After he has been dried off and warmed up a bit, Queequeg is quite casual about his heroism.

COMMENT

When the man's life is at stake, Queequeg forgets that the victim has insulted him only moments earlier, and risks his own life to save that of a man whom he might have considered his enemy. Fittingly, the ship's captain is forced to reverse judgment of Queequeg; he makes an apology to this noble "cannibal."

CHAPTER 14: NANTUCKET

The two companions arrive at Nantucket without further adventure. Ishmael reflects on the nature and the history of this barren island, and remarks that it is no wonder the Nantucketers took to the sea for a living. He especially concentrates his musings on the whale, "that Himmalehan, salt-sea Mastodon" of "unconscious power." Ishmael suggests that the Nantucketer alone lives out of the ocean proper, whereas most sailors and merchants merely use the sea as a means of transportation for goods that are essentially foreign to the ocean.

CHAPTER 15: CHOWDER
The packet boat arrives at Nantucket well after dark, creating difficulties for Ishmael and Queequeg in their search for the Try Pots, the inn that Peter Coffin has recommended to them. They find the place eventually, however, and the landlady brings them steaming bowls of clam and codfish chowder. The two friends go to bed after Queequeg has left his harpoon (a weapon with which one harpooneer committed suicide at the Try Pots) downstairs with the landlady.

CHAPTER 16: THE SHIP
Queequeg informs Ishmael that his idol, Yojo, has decided that Ishmael must choose the ship on which the two men shall sail. Ishmael does not care for the plan, but Queequeg refuses to run counter to Yojo's wishes, so the next morning, while Queequeg observes a day of fasting and prayer, Ishmael sets out to find a ship. There are three vessels preparing for long whaling voyages: the Devil-Dam, the Tit-Bit, and the Pequod. The Pequod (the name is that of a native American tribe massacred by the English Puritans) fascinates him because of its name and its ancient, noble appearance. Looking about the worn quarter-deck, Ishmael sees a little tent-like structure, in which he encounters Captain Peleg (another Bible name, which means "division"), a crotchety old man who is part owner of the Pequod. Peleg scoffs at Ishmael's limited experience as a merchant seaman, and asks if he has met Captain Ahab. Peleg explains that he and Captain Bildad own the Pequod, and will outfit her for sailing, but that Ahab will sail with her and be in charge throughout the voyage. He tells Ishmael that Ahab lost one leg in an encounter with "the monstrousest parmacetty [whale] that ever chipped a boat."

Ishmael next meets Captain Bildad (another Bible name, meaning "son of contention"), a quiet, unobtrusive, but cold person. Peleg rages briefly against Bildad's miserly proposal that Ishmael be given the seven hundred and seventy-seventh lay—that is, 1/777 of the profits from the voyage—and signs Ishmael on the crew for the three hundredth lay. Ishmael mentions Queequeg and his skill to Peleg, and Peleg tells him to bring the harpooneer down to the ship to sign up. As he is leaving, Ishmael asks to see Ahab, and is told that Ahab will not see anyone at present. Peleg tells Ishmael that Ahab is an extraordinary man and a hard taskmaster. Ishmael remembers that the Ahab of the Bible was an evil king. Peleg warns him never to mention the Biblical Ahab on board the Pequod. Captain Ahab did not name himself, and Peleg has sailed with him and knows that he is a good and pious man. However, Ahab has been moody, taciturn, and sometimes savage since the encounter with the whale and the loss of his leg. Ishmael departs, feeling a mixture of awe, sympathy, and wonder of Ahab.

COMMENT

Melville indirectly introduces Ahab through the conversation between Peleg and Ishmael. The reader learns that Ahab lost his leg to a whale, and that he has brooded on the accident ever since; that he is a good and pious man, though moody, and that he will be in charge of the ship throughout the voyage.

The Biblical references continue, as three more characters with names from the Bible are introduced. Ahab is named for a king of Israel who, at the request of his wife Jezebel, built a temple to Baal, a rival of God. King Ahab was also a thief and a murderer, and died in fulfillment of a curse. The names of both Peleg and Bildad suggest quarrel and strife.

CHAPTER 17: THE RAMADAN

Ishmael returns to the inn, but out of respect for Queequeg's Ramadan he decides not to disturb his friend until dark. When he knocks on the door at evening, Queequeg fails to answer, and the silence within continues even though Ishmael creates a disturbance, banging and shouting in the hallway. The landlady notices that Queequeg's harpoon is missing, and frantically concludes that he has killed himself. Ishmael breaks open the door, and finds Queequeg squatting in the middle of the floor with Yojo on his head. He will not respond to Ishmael's worried questions, nor does he do so at bedtime, when Ishmael asks him to take something to eat. Only when the sun shines into the room early next morning does Queequeg arise from this torturous position.

Ishmael, convinced that this behavior amounts to religious fanaticism, tries to persuade Queequeg that his practices are in error, but Queequeg can understand only a little of Ishmael's argument, and pays no attention to what he does understand. The two decide to live and let live, and go down to the ship after an unusually hearty breakfast.

CHAPTER 18: HIS MARK

As Ishmael and Queequeg approach the Pequod, Captain Peleg shouts that the savage will not be allowed aboard unless he can produce papers showing him to be a Christian. For a moment this seems an impossible difficulty, but Ishmael's earnest argument that Queequeg belongs to the original "ancient Catholic Church" ("catholic" means universal—in other words, Queequeg belongs not to a specific sect, but to the brotherhood of the human race) persuades the good-natured Peleg that, in this case, papers won't be necessary.

Peleg asks Queequeg if he has ever harpooned a whale. In answer, he leaps atop a bulwark, points to a tiny spot of tar on the water, and drives it under with a perfect "dart" or throw of his harpoon. Excited by such astounding skill, Peleg signs him on immediately, calling him Quohog (a type of clam common in Nantucket) rather than Queequeg. Queequeg does not sign his name in English writing, but "makes his mark"—copies the tattoo on his arm onto the contract.

CHAPTER 19: THE PROPHET

As Ishmael and Queequeg leave the Pequod, they are accosted by a shabby, wild-looking old man who asks them, "Shipmates, have ye shipped in that ship?" Ishmael admits that they have done so, whereupon the stranger reels off a series of incoherent but vaguely frightening remarks about what has happened to Ahab in the past, including the loss of his leg. Ishmael insists that the man come to the point but he is evasive, saying only "What's to be will be. . . . Morning to ye, shipmates, morning." Before they part, however, the old man tells Ishmael that his name is Elijah (the name of an Old Testament prophet). The man follows them for some time but finally disappears, and Ishmael concludes that he is a fraud.

COMMENT

Melville continues to develop the Biblical motif underlying the story. In the Bible, Elijah and Ahab were enemies. Elijah destroyed Ahab's temple to Baal and later put a curse on Ahab, which was partly fulfilled by Ahab's death.

Melville continues to build up suspense as he delays Ahab's first appearance in the novel. Elijah drops a number of mysterious hints about Ahab, and the reader's curiosity and apprehension grow.

CHAPTER 20: ALL ASTIR

Immense amounts of food, spare parts, and materials for repairs are taken aboard the Pequod, in preparation for a voyage of three years, as well as the barrels needed to store whale oil. Ishmael and Queequeg decide to remain ashore as long as possible, but visit the ship daily to observe the preparations. Ishmael is amused by the activity of Captain Bildad's sister, Aunt Charity, who brings aboard such items as jars of pickles. Ishmael asks about Ahab several times, but receives evasive answers. He experiences misgivings about sailing for three years under a man he has never seen. At last the ship is ready to sail.

CHAPTER 21: GOING ABOARD

At dawn, Ishmael and Queequeg approach the Pequod through the misty air. Ishmael notices some shadows, which seem to be sailors hurrying toward the ship. Suddenly Elijah appears out of the mist with a shout, asking if they plan to board the vessel. When Ishmael assures him that they do, Elijah asks how soon they plan to return, and implies that they may not come back at all. He tells them to see if they can find the four or five figures who boarded the ship a moment earlier, and then disappears with one last suggestion that they may not see each other again. Ishmael concludes that Elijah is "cracked," and he and Queequeg go on board and down to the forecastle, where they have a smoke. The fragrance of the smoke awakens a lone sleeper there, who tells them that Ahab has come aboard and has vanished into his cabin. Then the voice of Starbuck, the first mate, is heard, and soon seamen begin to arrive in twos and threes.

COMMENT

Elijah's appearance here reiterates his earlier ominous warning.

CHAPTER 22: MERRY CHRISTMAS

About noon, Captain Peleg tells Starbuck to order the men to their posts, and begins to order them about ferociously. Bildad, who will pilot the ship out of the harbor, stations himself at the bow to perform his chore. The anchor is raised and the Pequod heads toward open water. By dark the ship is well offshore, and Peleg and Bildad bid a slow, sentimental farewell to their ship and their friends. It is a freezing winter night as the ship plunges "like fate into the lone Atlantic."

CHAPTER 23: THE LEE SHORE

As the Pequod heads farther out to sea, Ishmael glances toward the stern to see who the helmsman is. To his astonishment, it is none other than Bulkington, the colossus who so interested him back at the Spouter-Inn. Here is a man who, like the ships he sails in, must avoid the shore.

COMMENT

Ishmael admires Bulkington for choosing the dangerous life of the sea and turning his back on a safe and comfortable life on land

CHAPTER 24: THE ADVOCATE

Ishmael plays advocate for the whaling industry in this chapter, hoping to demonstrate that it is as honorable a calling as any of the more respected professions. Whaling is butchery, it is true—but so is the highest military art, says Ishmael. Whaling has wide-reaching economic significance. Whalemen have led the world in the exploration of remote regions; they were the first to break through the despotism of Spain. Whaling has a literary history—whalemen have shown themselves to have "good blood"—the whale has been specially set aside as a "royal fish"—on and on Ishmael goes, defending the trade he loves and admires from would-be detractors. He ends by commenting that, if he should by chance leave a precious manuscript to the world after his death, all the credit should go to the whaling trade, for the whale-ship was his university.

CHAPTER 25: POSTSCRIPT

Ishmael adds one conjecture as an afterthought to the preceding "defense" of whaling: What kind of oil is used to anoint kings and queens at coronation ceremonies? What type could possibly be used but the noblest and sweetest of all, the natural oil of the sperm whale?

COMMENT

These two chapters recall the etymology and extracts with which the novel opens. They deal with the history of whales and whaling, as if the novel were a work of nonfiction. Chapters like 24 and 25 will alternate for the rest of the novel with narrative chapters.

CHAPTER 26: KNIGHTS AND SQUIRES

The first mate of the Pequod, Starbuck, is a thirty-year-old Quaker from Nantucket. He is a thin, leathery man of excellent health, tough and sturdy enough to adapt to any climate and to survive vast amounts of physical strain. He is extremely brave without being in the least foolhardy. Starbuck thinks, "I am here in this critical ocean to kill whales for my living, and not to be killed by them for theirs," and he acts upon this principle when in a whaleboat. He has a basic weakness despite his bravery, however: His devoutness tends toward superstition. He can conquer any physical fear, but he is the type of man, Ishmael tells us, who "cannot withstand those more terrific, because more spiritual terrors, which sometimes menace you from the concentrating brow of an enraged and mighty man."

COMMENT

Starbuck made a brief appearance earlier in the novel, during the Pequod's final preparations for sailing. Here, Ishmael gives us a detailed portrait of the first mate.

CHAPTER 27: KNIGHTS AND SQUIRES

The Pequod's second mate is a careless, good-natured man from Cape Cod named Stubb. Stubb is always smoking a pipe, even when about to harpoon a whale, and he dearly loves physical comfort. The third mate is a stocky, aggressive man named Flask, who comes from Martha's Vineyard. He is utterly without fear or respect for the whale; to him "the wondrous whale was but a species of magnified mouse." The three mates command the three whaleboats when the chase for whales is on. Ishmael compares each mate to a medieval knight who has a squire in attendance—the "squires" in this case being the harpooneers. Starbuck chooses Queequeg for his boat, Stubb chooses Tashtego, a native American from Gay Head (the west end of Martha's Vineyard), and Flask's harpooneer is Daggoo, an immense African. The rest of the crew consists of men from all over the world.

COMMENT

Melville's chapter title openly invites us to compare the mates and harpooneers—and the rest of the Pequod's complement—with the heroic characters of ancient romance and epic. The international crew loosely symbolizes mankind, and the ship is a kind of microcosm, a little world in itself.

CHAPTER 28: AHAB

Nothing is seen of the captain for some time after the Pequod puts out of Nantucket—he remains constantly in his cabin. Ishmael surveys the deck for Ahab, but never sees him until the ship is well south of the savage North Atlantic winter. Then one moderate morning Ahab appears on the quarter-deck. He is a big man, apparently in good health, who looks as though he were "made of solid bronze." Two physical deformities are evident: a tremendous, livid scar which runs down the side of his face, and a leg made of a whale's jaw-bone. He stands facing out over the ship's bow, "a crucifixion in his face, in all the nameless regal overbearing dignity of some mighty woe."

Every morning after this first appearance, Ahab can be seen by the crew, sitting, standing, or pacing on his quarter-deck. Eventually the weather becomes so fine as to chase away some of the many clouds that Ishmael notices on Ahab's brow.

COMMENT

Melville built up tension by keeping Ahab out of the

novel for so long, and Ahab's first appearance is dramatic. Melville does not weaken the effect by having Ahab do or say anything: His mere presence is potent enough. Ishmael's description of Ahab's face is a powerful characterization.

CHAPTER 29: ENTER AHAB; TO HIM, STUBB

As the days roll by, the weather becomes truly beautiful. Ahab is tormented by sleeplessness and spends most of the nights on deck. Forgetting one night that his three mates sleep immediately below the quarter deck, he begins to pace restlessly and awakens Stubb, who ascends and humorously suggests that Ahab's thumping ivory leg might be muffled. Ahab, enraged, berates him and snarls, "Down, dog, and kennel!" Stubb reacts in anger, but for a reason he cannot fathom—certainly not from fear—he retreats back to his cabin and wonders whether he should mount up to the deck again and strike Ahab, or get down on his knees and pray for him. He muses on a remark made by the cabin boy that Ahab's hammock is frightfully hot in the morning, and assumes that Ahab has "what some folks ashore call a conscience." He also wonders why Ahab goes down into the cargo hold every night.

COMMENT

For the first time in the novel, Melville shifts the narrating voice. Ishmael does not narrate this chapter; he has been replaced by an omniscient third-person narrator, who can overhear both Ahab and Stubb talking to themselves. The chapter title is written as if it were a stage direction.

MOBY-DICK
CHAPTERS 30–45

CHAPTER 30: THE PIPE

After Stubbs' departure, Ahab leans on the railing for a while, then decides to have a smoke. He lights his pipe and puffs on it for a few minutes, then realizes that he no longer derives any pleasure from smoking. Remarking that his condition is sad indeed when he can't enjoy his pipe, he throws it into the sea. It hisses and disappears.

COMMENT

Ahab is well aware of his own unhappiness, and denies himself any small comfort that might cheer him up.

CHAPTER 31: QUEEN MAB

Stubb tells Flask about an odd dream he had after the incident with Ahab. Ahab kicked him with his ivory leg, and when Stubb attempted to return the kick, his leg came off. An old man came along and interfered, and Stubb, annoyed, threatened to kick him. The old man turned around and showed a rump full of marlinspikes. Stubb wisely decided not to kick so formidable a person. The old man told Stubb that he should feel honored to be kicked by Ahab, who has a leg of genuine ivory rather than a common wooden leg. Flask is bewildered by the dream, and Stubb concludes that it is not wise to argue with Ahab. At this point Ahab calls out that there are whales in the vicinity, and tells the crew to look especially for a white whale. Stubb shakes his head, realizing that Ahab "has that that's bloody on his mind."

COMMENT

Queen Mab is a Celtic name for the queen of the fairies, who rules the dreams of human beings. In Act I Scene 4 of Shakespeare's Romeo and Juliet, Mercutio tells Romeo about Queen Mab in a lengthy and beautiful monologue.

Stubb addresses the old man in the dream as "Mr. Humpback." A humpback is a type of whale. Since the old man's body is stuffed with marlinspikes, he may well symbolize a whale: Whales that have been wounded but not killed often carry pieces of harpoons in their bodies. "Mr. Humpback" also believes it is an honor to be injured with an ivory weapon; whales' chief weapons, of course, are their ivory teeth.

Ahab's mention of the white whale is his first direct reference to Moby Dick. Moby Dick has yet to be named in the novel, but Melville has dropped a few specific clues about him. He is gigantic, even for a whale, and white where most whales are dark in color.

The omniscient third-person narrator first heard in Chapter 29 narrates this chapter as well. Ishmael would not have overheard the conversation between Stubb and Flask.

CHAPTER 32: CETOLOGY

Ishmael decides to provide us with some sound general background about whales. He points out that little has been written about the whale, and much of that is inaccurate. He first defines a whale as "a spouting fish with a horizontal tail," scoffing at those who consider it a mammal. Then Ishmael divides all whales into three "books": folio, octavo, and duodecimo. (These names refer to different standard sizes in which books are made. The folio is the largest size. The octavo and the duodecimo are respectively one-eighth and one-twelfth the size of a folio.) Ishmael discusses the name, appearance and characteristics of fourteen types of whales within these three size categories. He ends his discussion of cetology—for the time being—with a reference to a group of whales he considers to be fictitious.

COMMENT

Ishmael objects to the name "killer whale" on the grounds that all things kill to live and a particular whale should

not be singled out as being in any way morally more
guilty than other species.

Recall that the etymology was supplied by a man who
worked in a grammar school; that the extracts were
supplied by a "sub-sub-librarian"; and that the entire
novel is permeated by references to the whale and
descriptions of the whale's body. Melville is apparently
trying to make the "stuff" of the whale the "stuff" of the
book. In this attempt he is following a principle
precious to several of his major contemporaries, nota-
bly Emerson, Thoreau, and Whitman, called the "organic
principle." These writers attempted to make the form of
their works reflect their contents as directly and sponta-
neously as possible. Melville's grammarian and librarian
and Ishmael's extended metaphor of whales as books
seem intended to stress the direct connection between
the whale as actuality and the whale as it can be
presented through language.

CHAPTER 33: THE SPECKSYNDER

Ishmael gives us some information about the relationship
between officers and men on a whaleship. The officers sleep
toward the stern, the crewmen forward. But the harpooneers
are an exception because of their special importance to the
success of the voyage, and long usage dictates that they will
sleep just forward of the captain and mates. Their importance
is such that in the early days of whaling a special title,
Specksynder (a Dutch word meaning Fat-Cutter) was given to
the chief harpooneer. The Specksynder's function was to over-
see all whale-hunting activities, while the captain was limited
to the general command of the ship proper.

Ishmael explains that, because a whaler depends for its
success upon the hard work of all crewmen, a democratic
slackening of rigid shipboard discipline is sometimes found
in the whaling fleet. Ahab, for instance, although he expects

instant, unquestioning obedience from all his men, demands little from them in the way of formalities. Nevertheless, says Ishmael, he is not above taking advantage of his crew's traditional obedience for his own private ends. Ishmael concludes that no man in this world can successfully command other men without the use of "arts and entrenchments," which are "paltry and base."

COMMENT

Besides stressing the distinctions between officers and men and the importance of the harpooneers, this chapter hints obliquely at Ahab's hidden motives, about which Melville has already suggested some clues to the reader.

Ishmael's comments about the basic immorality of men ruling over other men recall his words in Chapter 1, as he explained his habit of shipping as a common sailor.

CHAPTER 34: THE CABIN-TABLE

This chapter explains the tradition of the captain and his three mates dining together, and the laws of precedence which apply. Ahab enters the cabin and seats himself, followed in rank order by Starbuck, Stubb, and Flask. Becasue they leave in reverse order, Flask often has to bolt his dinner as fast as possible. He feels that he has never had a full meal since he became an officer. Ahab is moody and silent throughout meals, and the mates must respect his silence and not talk either.

The three harpooners dine after the captain leaves the cabin and the table has been reset. Queequeg, Daggoo, and Tashtego are lively, loud, and sociable during their meals, forming a strong contrast to the silent officers. However, neither the harpooners nor the three mates enter the cabin except for meals. The cabin is considered by all to be Ahab's private property, and his manner is too moody and aloof to invite trespassers.

CHAPTER 35: THE MAST-HEAD

Ishmael tells us that his first turn to stand watch at the mast-heads comes during very pleasant weather. The function of the mast-head watch is to keep a lookout for whales, and an American whaleship usually mans the mast-head from the time it leaves port until its very last barrel is filled with whale oil. Generally, standing mast-head watches is completely uneventful in such a peaceful sea as the South Pacific, Ishmael informs us. The only great inconvenience lies in the fact that American whalers have no crow's nest, and the watch must stand perched precariously on the narrow crosstrees high up the mast.

Ishmael starts thinking about lookouts in history who had nothing to do with whaling: Egyptian astronomers, Saint Simon Stylites (the Christian hermit who lived atop a rock pillar), Washington, and Napoleon. Ishmael admits that he does not make a good sentry, because the solitude and the unbroken view of the sea encourage him to get lost in his own thoughts.

COMMENT

Once again, Ishmael connects the operations of whaling with the whole history of mankind, this time suggesting a vague connection between standing a mast-head and reaching, whether successfully or not, for almost superhuman achievements.

CHAPTER 36: THE QUARTER-DECK

One morning, not long after he has thrown away his pipe, Ahab paces the deck more restlessly and intensely than usual. That evening, he orders Starbuck to command all the men aft—an extraordinary event on shipboard. When the crew is assembled, Ahab asks them what they do when they see a whale—and what next?—and after that? The men shout their answers as Ahab's nervous energy transmits itself to them. When he has them thoroughly excited, Ahab suddenly produces a doubloon (a sixteen-dollar gold piece), nails it to a mainmast, and announces that it will become the property of the first man to sight a certain white whale. Tashtego asks if this whale is Moby Dick: Daggoo and Queequeg have also seen Moby Dick, and describe his bushy spout, his swimming habits, and the bits of harpoons that are stuck in his body.

Starbuck asks Ahab if Moby Dick is the whale that tore his leg off. Ahab says that he is, and that he will chase him "round perdition's flames" for revenge: This is the motive of the Pequod's voyage. Starbuck objects that vengeance against an animal who did no intentional evil seems blasphemous. Ahab cries out that he is convinced that, through Moby Dick, evil has injured him, and he is determined on his revenge. He calls the steward for a large tankard and has the three harpooners and all the crew drink from it, swearing, "Death to Moby Dick!" as they do so. Starbuck is disturbed and Stubb and Flask uncomfortable.

COMMENT

In this chapter, Melville reveals the novel's major conflict and the main thread of its plot: Ahab's desire for revenge, and his pursuit of Moby Dick.

Ahab leads the men to the precise pitch of excitement that he desires. His overbearing personality is here brought into play for the first time, along with his flair for the dramatic.

CHAPTER 37: SUNSET

Ahab sits in his cabin, watching the wake of the Pequod and contemplating the sinking sun. He considers the torment of his driving urge to destroy Moby Dick, and regrets that he can no longer enjoy the beauty of the sunset. Then he ponders the ease with which he persuaded the crew, with the exception of Starbuck, to join wholeheartedly in the quest for Moby Dick. He remembers the prophecy that he would lose his leg, and now he prophesies that he will "dismember the dismemberer." He is determined never to be swayed from his purpose.

COMMENT

Once again, Melville shifts the narrating voice. This chapter is presented as if it were a soliloquy in a play. The chapter begins with a stage direction: "The cabin; by the stern windows; Ahab sitting alone, and gazing out." Ahab speaks throughout in the first person. This choice allows Melville to present Ahab's thoughts unedited by any narrator, which makes them more immediate, powerful, and direct. Here we see Ahab's own point of view, after the preceding chapters gave us Ishmael's and others' views of him.

Ahab's soliloquy tells the reader that he takes no pleasure in his quest for revenge. He mourns his inability to feel the beauty of the sunset; he feels that he is "damned in the midst of Paradise." He makes the voyage on the Pequod not because he wants revenge, but because he has chosen to go after revenge, and is determined to succeed. "What I've dared, I've willed; and what I've willed, I'll do!" he vows.

CHAPTER 38: DUSK

Starbuck, leaning against the mainmast, reflects on Ahab's triumph over the crew. He feels that Ahab is a madman, but admits that Ahab is his captain and he must obey him and help him in his quest for revenge. Starbuck deeply pities Ahab's madness. He is distressed at the "heathenish" behavior of the crew and their zest for the chase after Moby Dick. He prays for help to get through the voyage.

COMMENT

Like the previous chapter, "Dusk" is a soliloquy, opening with a stage direction. The reader is allowed to see Starbuck's thoughts exactly as he thinks them, without the filter of another character's interpretation.

This soliloquy makes it clear that Starbuck is deeply distressed over the situation on board the Pequod. He fears Ahab's madness and sincerely pities him, and he feels that he is helpless to do anything other than obey Ahab. He prays for help.

CHAPTER 39: FIRST NIGHT-WATCH

Stubb stands alone at the foremast, mending a brace. He wonders about the Pequod's future, and decides that the best thing to do is to laugh off the problem. No matter what happens, he will take comfort in his belief that the future is predetermined, and man can do nothing about it.

COMMENT

This chapter is the third soliloquy in a row. Like Ahab's and Starbuck's, Stubb's soliloquy is entirely characteristic of him. He is not just thinking, but doing something while he thinks; and he does not think too deeply into the matter, but decides it will work itself out without his interference.

CHAPTER 40: MIDNIGHT, FORECASTLE

The seamen and harpooneers are gathered together in the crew's quarters. The men are carousing; they have been drinking, and are dancing and singing in a dangerously playful mood. As the revelry continues a storm blows up. A Spanish sailor insults Daggoo and the two are about to brawl when one of the mates calls all hands aloft to take in sails (so that the raging storm will not tear them away.) Pip, the Caribbean cabin-boy, is frightened of the storm and also of the drunken men.

COMMENT

Melville continues his dramatic narration. This chapter is written out like a scene in a play, with character's names appearing before their speeches. The "scene" includes several stage directions, and introduces a number of new characters. Most have names such as "1st Nantucket Sailor" or "Spanish Sailor," but one new character, Pip, has his own name. Pip's fear of the storm foreshadows his fall into madness later in the novel.

Note that Ishmael does not appear in this scene. Since the beginning of the voyage, Ishmael has not been involved in any of the action. He has stood off to one side, recording his impressions for the reader.

This chapter presents a number of parallelisms between the unrest aboard the Pequod and the unrest of nature. A few examples are:
1) The white lightning in the sky is compared to Ahab's scar.
2) The fight in the forecastle is compared to the storm in the sky. Tashtego says, "Gods and men—both brawlers!"
3) The ring formed for the fight between the Spaniard and Daggoo is paralleled to "the ringed horizon" by the old Manxman. He says, "In that ring Cain struck Abel," suggesting that men have violated the idea of brotherhood since the beginning of time.

CHAPTER 41: MOBY DICK

Ishmael explains the whaler's belief that sperm whales are the largest and fiercest of all whales, and that even among sperm whales, Moby Dick is exceptional. He has maimed or killed many of his pursuers, so that those who have met him (except for Ahab) hope to avoid him in the future. After Ahab tells the crew about the real object of the Pequod's voyage, Ishmael tries to find out as much as he can about Moby Dick from the other sailors.

Moby Dick is much larger than most sperm whales. He has a snow-white forehead, a high white hump on his back, and a deformed, scythe-like lower jaw. Most striking of all, he seems to attack whalers deliberately and maliciously, which terrifies many of the men who have battled him. Among others who have suffered because of this apparent maliciousness is Ahab, who, trying to kill Moby Dick with a mere knife, lost his leg. Ishmael suggests that Ahab developed his abiding hatred for the whale not immediately, but in long months of anguished brooding. Ahab came to believe that Moby Dick symbolized all the evil in the world, and is determined to pursue him and kill him. Ishmael comments that the Pequod's crew of "mongrel renegades, castaways, and cannibals" is perfectly chosen for Ahab's purpose.

COMMENT
In this chapter, Melville finally gives the reader a detailed, specific portrait of Moby Dick; his physical appearance, his personality as it appears to the whaling community, and exactly what occurred between him and Ahab.

CHAPTER 42: THE WHITENESS OF THE WHALE
Ishmael tells us that, for him, Moby Dick's most appalling characteristic was his white color. He tries to explain why this should be so. First, he considers whiteness in general: it adds beauty to many natural objects (such as marble); it is often connected with royalty; it is frequently a symbol of joy; in several religions it is symbolic of the greatest purity and power— yet for all these good and noble connotations, there is still a vague "something" about whiteness that is frightening. Next Ishmael reflects on whiteness in animals: the polar bear and the white shark are especially terrifying; the albatross is linked to several superstitious fears; the albino horse, the "White Squall" of the Pacific, and the whiteness of the dead all have especially disturbing aspects. Why is all this so? Because white-ness itself is somehow frightening. The bravest man, when shrouded in a white fog at sea, or surrounded by ice and snow in the Antarctic, will feel an unnamed fear grasp him.

CHAPTER 43: HARK!

One quiet night, a group of seamen are passing buckets of water from the large storage barrel amidships to the smaller barrel on the quarter-deck. Archy suddenly hisses to his neighbor, "Did you hear that noise, Cabaco?" Cabaco hears nothing, but Archy insists that he heard a cough from the after-hold, where no one should be quartered. There is a stowaway hiding down there, he feels, and Ahab knows of it.

COMMENT

Melville gives the reader another mystery to wonder about. Remember the "shadows" Ishmael thought he saw when boarding the ship in Chapter 21, and Elijah's suggestion that he should look for them once he boards the ship.

CHAPTER 44: THE CHART

This chapter picks up the narration after the storm that hit the Pequod in Chapter 40. Ahab goes to his cabin, takes out his roll of yellowed old sea charts and slowly traces lines here and there, marking places where sperm whales have been found at different seasons of the year. Ahab is charting the courses on which he is most likely to encounter Moby Dick. Because whales tend to swim in veins (long paths a few miles wide, which they follow by instinct), Ahab's hopes of meeting Moby Dick somewhere in the South Pacific are not actually far-fetched. As Ahab works, the swinging lamp above his head throws highlights and shadows on his forehead, "till it almost seemed that while he himself was marking out lines and courses on the wrinkled charts, some invisible pencil was also tracing lines and courses upon the deeply marked chart of his forehead." Ishmael comments that, like any man bent on a fixed purpose of revenge, Ahab does not sleep well. He has many nightmares, and often cries out in the night and comes out on deck for some air.

COMMENT

Ahab's obsession with the whale is made even clearer by what he does in this chapter. The images, as well as the action of the chapter, emphasize this obsession. The chart is very deliberately paralleled with Ahab's forehead in the second paragraph. The lines on the chart that the whale follows are like the lines that Ahab's quest has engraved on his forehead; the whale may be said to "swim" in Ahab's veins as it swims in the veins in the ocean. But the whale in the ocean is a gigantic animal; the whale in the world of Ahab's brain is a demon.

The description of Ahab's nightmares is full of words like hell, fiends, demons, and fire. Melville implies that Ahab has made his own hell and will suffer in it until his quest is settled one way or the other.

CHAPTER 45: THE AFFIDAVIT

Ishmael substantiates the comments he has made concerning the possibility of one man's encountering the same whale twice. He knows of three instances in which a man has killed a whale and found his own old harpoons imbedded in the whale's flesh. Further, individual sperm whales like Moby Dick are recognizable to the whaling fleet at large, usually because of reputations for violence. Rinaldo Rinaldini, Timor Jack, and New Zealand Tom were three whales who literally made names for themselves by their behavior. Ishmael also wants to prove that his descriptions of the terrifying powers of the whale are not exaggerated, but factual. He mentions first that, although few outside the whaling industry know it, most whaleships lose one man or more per voyage. Second, says Ishmael, a sperm whale may actually be heavy and powerful enough to sink a ship! He cites examples of a whaler and a warship that were rammed by sperm whales: the former sank and the latter had to be repaired. Other instances of the whale's immense power are given, such as the case of the small sloop, which was lifted out of the water on a whale's back, and several incidents in which full-sized ships were towed by harpooned sperm whales.

COMMENT

As in the "Extracts" and elsewhere, Ishmael piles up examples, some factual and some conjectural, from a wide variety of times and places.

With these general remarks about whales, Melville continues to build up a portrait of Moby Dick for the reader. Chapters like this one explain Moby Dick's habits, his reputation for violence, exactly what that violence consists of, and what his relationship is to whalers in general.

MOBY-DICK
CHAPTERS 46–63

CHAPTER 46: SURMISES

Ahab, though burning with the desire to meet Moby Dick, urges his crew to keep a sharp watch for all whales. He has several reasons for doing this. He wants to keep the men in practice for his ultimate goal, Moby Dick; he must keep Starbuck busy to prevent him from rebelling against Ahab's quest; he wants to prevent "the full terror of the voyage" from engaging the men's superstitious imaginations; he wants to keep the crew's crude appetite for excitement well satisfied. Furthermore, his vengeance against Moby Dick amounts to stealing the Pequod from its owners in order to use it for his own purposes; the crew, in this situation, has the right to mutiny. Therefore he will obscure the eventual aim of the voyage, as far as he can, by running the ship as if it were on an ordinary whaling cruise.

COMMENT

The narrating voice shifts again, from Ishmael to an omniscient third-person narrator. Ishmael would only be able to guess at Ahab's motives: the omniscient narrator can present them to the reader as facts rather than guesses or opinions.

CHAPTER 47: THE MAT-MAKER

Ishmael and Queequeg are working together one hot, cloudy afternoon, weaving a mat of crude yarns. Ishmael muses on their task: He fancies that he is weaving his own destiny, made up of free will, chance, and fate. Suddenly, Ishmael is startled out of his daydreams by an unearthly cry from Tashtego, at the masthead: "There she blows!" He has sighted a school of whales, and a wild flurry of activity follows. The whaleboats are swung over the sides, and all hands are poised to swing into action as soon as the whales come to the surface after their dive. At this tense moment a shout is heard; all hands glance at Ahab, and, amazed, they see him surrounded by "five dusky phantoms that seemed fresh formed out of air."

COMMENT

The "five phantoms" who appear here are the "shadows" Ishmael saw through the mist at Nantucket. They are also the source of the mysterious cough of Chapter 43. Notice that Melville, calling them "shadows" and "phantoms," stresses their insubstantiality.

CHAPTER 48: THE FIRST LOWERING

The "phantoms" prove to be the crew for Ahab's own whaleboat. His harpooner is Fedallah, a white-haired man of Asian appearance; the other four are Philippine sailors. Ahab orders the three boats of the mates to drop into the sea and pull away, but they hesitate, looking at Fedallah in puzzlement. Starbuck starts to question Ahab, but Ahab repeats his orders and the boats row after the whales, Ahab's boat following. As they race after the whales, the crews and officers discuss the new crew members; no one likes the situation, but all agree it can't be helped. The boats catch up to the whales just as a storm breaks. In Starbuck's boat (in which Ishmael is rowing) Queequeg darts his harpoon at a whale as wind and waves overturn the boat. The boat, though swamped, is unharmed, and the men spend a miserable night in it, rocking on a rough sea. At dawn the Pequod suddenly bears down on them out of the fog. They leap for their lives as the ship grinds over the whaleboat, and are picked up a few minutes later.

COMMENT

This chapter is Ishmael's introduction to the actualities of whaling. Besides being an intensely exciting "action" episode, it presents us with a view of the deadly dangers of whaling, and also conveys ominous suggestions for the future.

The identity of the shadows Ishmael saw, and the stowaways Archy heard coughing, is revealed. Ahab has smuggled a harpooner and a crew of his own on board.

CHAPTER 49: THE HYENA

There are times, Ishmael avers, when life seems a colossal practical joke. Such a time is likely to come at a moment of extreme peril, such as the crisis through which Ishmael has just passed during the first lowering. He asks Queequeg, Stubb, and Flask if the kind of danger he has just encountered is common in whaling, and he is assured by each in turn that it is very common indeed. Considering the various pitfalls awaiting him during the rest of the voyage—the general danger of whaling, the added dangers of storm and sea, and the very special danger involved in hunting Moby Dick—Ishmael decides that the most prudent thing to do is to go below and make out his will. Queequeg acts as witness for the will, as well as beneficiary.

Ishmael adds that it may seem odd to the reader that sailors should be fond of making wills, but such is the case. This will is the fourth that Ishmael has made.

CHAPTER 50: AHAB'S BOAT AND CREW—FEDALLAH

Stubb and Flask discuss the remarkable fact that Ahab went out in a whaleboat. Stubb thinks Ahab's daring is wonderful, but the unimaginative Flask is not impressed: Ahab's leg is not off at the hip, but at the knee, so there is little to admire in his feat!

Ishmael tells us that whalemen often argue about whether the captain should go out in a whaleboat. In Ahab's case the risk is intensified by his disability, and it is certain that the Pequod's owners would not want him to chase whales personally. This is why Ahab provided himself with a crew secretly, and took personal care in readying a boat for his own needs. The crew is odd, but no more peculiar than many a group that has assembled aboard a whaler, so they blend in with the rest of the Pequod's crew quickly enough—except for the harpooner, Fedallah. He remains a mystery, especially in that he seems to have some undefinable influence upon Ahab. Ishmael cannot say where he came from; he thinks Fedallah looks Asian, but, remembering myths of gods mating with human women, speculates that devils may do the same, and that Fedallah may be part human and part devil.

CHAPTER 51: THE SPIRIT-SPOUT

The Pequod sails southward peacefully for weeks, with no further sight of whales. One serene moonlight night, however, the silence is broken by Fedallah's cry: "There she blows!" He has spied a silvery spout far ahead in the midnight sea from his perch on the mainmast. Although, as Ishmael tells us, "Not one whaleman in a hundred would venture a lowering" at night, Ahab gives chase with all sails crowded on the Pequod's masts. But the spout is seen no more that night. Several nights later the spout is seen again and pursued, with the same result. It is seen frequently over the next several nights, but the Pequod never gets near it. The superstitious seamen fear that the spout is Moby Dick's, luring them onward toward destruction.

Soon the ship reaches the Cape of Good Hope (notorious for terrible weather), and for days fights its way through savage wind and waves. Sea birds perch in swarms in the rigging, and strange forms swim in the water around the Pequod. Ishmael suggests that condemned souls may be animating the sea creatures that the ship encounters. During the passage around the Cape, Ahab spends a great deal of time on deck, both day and night, looking doggedly ahead toward his goal in the teeth of the worst storms.

COMMENT

The description of the passage around Cape Horn is gripping, even though no real action takes place in this

chapter. More important, however, are two other aspects:
1) The fact that a "spirit spout" which may be Moby
Dick's leads the Pequod from serene seas into the
savage weather of the Cape is suggestive of dangers
ahead.

2) Ahab's furious determination is understood by his
remaining on deck, seemingly endlessly, in such foul
weather.

CHAPTER 52: THE ALBATROSS

As the Pequod heads toward the Indian Ocean after rounding
Africa, it encounters another ship named the Goney, or
Albatross. Its name seems appropriate, for, like the bird whose
name it bears, it is a bleached and faded white, with salt spray
caked all over it after a long whaling cruise. The two ships
pass so close to each other that their swaying mastheads
almost touch, but no word is spoken by the lookouts. Down
on the deck, Ahab calls to the Goney: "Ship ahoy! Have ye
seen the White Whale?" As the other captain prepares to shout
a reply, his speaking trumpet slips from his hand into the sea,
and his unaided voice cannot be heard over the rising wind
as the ships move farther and farther apart. Ahab considers
lowering a boat and trying to board the Goney, but the winds
are too high to attempt it. The seamen of the Pequod eye
each other silently because of this ominous accident at the
simple mention of Moby Dick to another ship. As the wakes
of the two ships cross, a school of little fish that has been
following the Pequod for several days races to the sides of the
Goney. Ahab, peering down into the water, is heard to
murmur sadly, "Swim away from me, do ye?"

COMMENT

The meeting with the Goney is the Pequod's first
encounter with another whaling ship. The Goney may
or may not have met Moby Dick on its voyage; it cannot
communicate with the Pequod, due to loss of the speaking trumpet and the winds.

CHAPTER 53: THE GAM

Picking up on the theme of the previous chapter, Ishmael explains that when two whalers meet in the untold thousands of miles of the ocean, they always stop for a brief visit with one another. These social visits, called gams, usually consist of a meeting between the two captains on one boat and the two chief mates on the other, with an interchange of news and information about whaling, and perhaps the exchange of letters or packages. Those at home can send mail by giving it to an outward-bound whaler, and sailors, in turn, can send letters by a ship they meet that is bound for home. However, Ishmael notices that Ahab shows no interest in a gam with a chance-met whaler, unless that ship can give him news of Moby Dick.

COMMENT

Ahab has left the land behind him in his zeal to kill the White whale; now he begins to ignore the society of the sea, too, if it has no bearing on his quest.

CHAPTER 54: THE TOWN-HO'S STORY

Shortly after meeting the Goney, the Pequod has a gam with another whaler, the Town-Ho. Three of the Town-Ho's men told the story of their encounter with Moby Dick to Tashtego, who eventually told it to others of the Pequod's crew. Ahab and the three mates never hear the story, because the Town-Ho's captain and mates do not know some parts of it. Ishmael tells it as he repeated it long afterwards to two young men on a sociable evening in Lima.

The Town-Ho, a Nantucket whaler cruising the Pacific, sprang a leak that, while not serious, required that her pumps be manned a couple of hours a day. The chief mate, the disagreeable and ugly Radney, hated Steelkilt, the handsome and popular leader of one of the pumping gangs. One evening, out of sheer spite, Radney ordered the exhausted Steelkilt to do a menial job that was not his duty. When Steelkilt refused, the mate threatened him with a hammer, and when the hammer grazed Steelkilt's cheek, he crushed Radney's jaw with one terrific punch. The officers immediately tried to subdue Steelkilt, but he and several others fought their way up to the forecastle deck, set up a barricade, and refused to return to work until the captain promised that there would be no punishment. Their demand was refused, whereupon they voluntarily accepted imprisonment in the hold. Eventually they gave up one by one, until only Steelkilt and two others were left; then the last two betrayed the fact that Steelkilt planned to mutiny. The two were flogged, but because of something Steelkilt whispered, the captain decided not to whip him. However, the cowardly Radney stepped forward and, despite Steelkilt's threats, flogged him.

After this episode things appeared to return to normal, but actually Steelkilt was planning to murder Radney in the middle of some night watch. Just as Steelkilt was creeping up on Radney to smash his skull and heave him overboard, a cry came from the masthead that a gigantic whale was in sight. The boats dropped into the sea and gave chase to the whale—Moby Dick. Radney's boat harpooned him, but as the whaleboat approached, Moby Dick bumped it, spilling Radney into the sea. In a fury, Moby Dick seized Radney in his jaws and mangled him. The boats chased Moby Dick again, but could not catch him, so they returned to the ship. At the first harbor, Steelkilt and most of the others deserted the Town-Ho, and the captain was forced to recruit Tahitians for the rest of the voyage.

COMMENT

In this story, Moby Dick appears as an instrument of divine justice, murdering the villainous Radney. The story supports the idea that Moby Dick has superhuman knowledge and power, but in this case he intervenes on the side of justice. The reader wonders again if Ahab's vengeance is misplaced. It is significant that Ahab never learns of Moby Dick's intervention against the evil Radney.

This chapter contains the basic plot and conflicts that Melville would later develop into the short novel *Billy Budd*—a handsome and popular sailor, an unpopular mate who unreasonably disliked and tried to make trouble for him, the sailor's physical attack on the mate, and a captain who attempted to handle the matter justly.

Meville chose to narrate this story, not as it happened in the course of the Pequod's voyage, but as Ishmael repeated it to some friends on land, much later, during a pleasant sociable evening. This detatches the episode from the rest of the novel, and allows the reader to enjoy it, surrounded by the festive atmosphere of Ishmael and his friends Pedro and Sebastian, without the suspense and anxiety that surround the Pequod's voyage.

CHAPTER 55: OF THE MONSTROUS PICTURES OF WHALES

Ishmael says that since he is soon going to give us a vivid and realistic portrait of the whale; he will first give us a view of some of the distorted pictures of him in the arts, sciences, and general life. The oldest of these fantastic representations are in Hindu, Egyptian, and Greek sculptures. (The oldest of all, representing the whale as half man, is in a cavern-pagoda in India.) But Guido's picture of the whale (early seventeenth-century Italian), Hogarth's (eighteenth-century English), and others by other artists are hardly more accurate. Among the pictures of whales produced by whalers and scientists, there are hardly any better representations: the flukes are vertical instead of horizontal, or the whale itself looks like a log, or a squash, or, in one case, "much like an amputated sow." And what of the popular pictures of whales on signs outside oil-dealers' shops? Worse yet. However, these mistakes are understandable, says Ishmael, for the only way one can really see the whale is while he is surging along in the ocean, and then most of him is out of sight. Only by going whaling can one get much of an idea of what leviathan truly is—and then the danger is so great that it might be better not to be too curious about the whale, after all.

CHAPTER 56: OF THE LESS ERRONEOUS PICTURES OF WHALES, AND THE TRUE PICTURES OF WHALING SCENES

After attacking grotesque portraits of the whale, Ishmael admits that there have been a few good reproductions of the whale's appearance. He knows of only four books on the sperm whale, of which Beale's is the best, especially for the pictures. But by far the finest portrayals of whales and whaling are two by Garney and two by Durand—both Frenchmen. They catch the whale himself fairly well, but better, they convey excellently the tremendous power of the whale and the intense excitement of the chase. By contrast, English and American works (though the product of better information) are mechanical and lifeless.

COMMENT

To Ishmael, the most important facet of portraying the whale is to show its colossal power and vitality. The whale's essence seems to him to be pulsing, developing reality, not mere size.

CHAPTER 57: OF WHALES IN PAINT; IN TEETH; IN WOOD; IN SHEET-IRON; IN STONE; IN MOUNTAINS; IN STARS

Some of the best representations of whales, Ishmael assures us, are done by sailors who carve them out of wood, teeth, and other materials. Other replicas, perhaps not so faithful to the originals, can be seen on door-knockers and weather vanes. Startling resemblances are sometimes found in oddly shaped rocks, or the tops of mountainous ridges in distant countries.

But the most striking "whale pictures" of all are the ones the man of imagination can see in the stars, constellation-like. Ishmael wishes he could ride the backs of such starry whales to examine the far heavens.

CHAPTER 58: BRIT

The Pequod sails through an immense patch of brit floating on the ocean. Brit is a tiny yellow stuff that looks like wheat; it is the primary food of the right whale. Numbers of these whales are seen swimming along, gathering quantities of brit in their open mouths. The Pequod chases only sperm whales, so the right whales swim beside her in perfect safety.

Ishmael reflects upon the fact that landsmen regard sea creatures as generally repulsive, and the sea itself as an eternal mystery. The sea is the enemy, not only of man, but of its own creatures as well. It is a subtle, treacherous, "universal cannibal," "all whose creatures prey upon each other."

CHAPTER 59: SQUID

Placidly the Pequod sails through the fields of brit. The mysterious silvery spout is still seen from time to time at night. One beautiful morning Daggoo sees a huge white mass rise once, twice, three times from the sea. He cries out that Moby Dick is breaching in front of them, and Ahab quickly launches all four boats on the calm sea. The white mass slowly rises once more, and the men stare in awe at the immense, cream-colored blob in front of them. Flask calls from his boat to ask Starbuck what it is, and Starbuck announces shakily that this is the great white squid, a creature universally regarded as an ill omen among whalemen.

Ishmael tells us that the great squid is rarely seen, and that it is evidently a major source of food for the sperm whale. Apparently the squid clings to the bottom of the ocean, and the sperm whale tears it loose from the sea floor with its powerful jaws. Arms of the squid have sometimes been disgorged by sperm whales when they were being pursued by whaleboats.

COMMENT

Notice how skillfully Melville creates an ominous, unreal tone in the entire passage describing the occurrence itself, then breaks this tone with the relatively matter-of-fact discussion of the squid as food.

CHAPTER 60: THE LINE

Ishmael describes the whale-line to us, because he is going to refer to it more than once in the future. It is made of soft, golden Manilla rope, two-thirds of an inch thick and 1,200 feet long, and will withstand a pull equal to almost three tons. It is coiled with extreme care into a tub about three feet in diameter and covered so as to resemble "a prodigious great wedding-cake" for the whales. The lower end is left loose, and has a large loop in it. Thus the line can be attached to a second one from another boat if the whale sounds (dives) too deep, or, if need be, the whale can simply carry off the loose line, rather than pulling the whaleboat under with it. At the other end of the line, two harpoons are attached by means of a rope called the short-warp.

Ishmael makes it clear why such care is employed in coiling the line. To give the rope some slack, it is passed back from the tub in the bow, around a "logger-head" (a short post) at the stern of the little whaleboat, and back up to the bow again. As it goes back, it rests on the oar handles on one side of the boat, just inside the oarsmen, and as it comes forward again, it rests on the oar handles on the other side. Thus the slightest kink might well mean the end of one or all in the boat.

COMMENT

Again, Ishmael stresses the dangers of whaling. Even more significant, he reflects that "all men live enveloped in whale-lines"—in one way or another, we are all at the mercy of fate, in imminent danger of death. Once again, whaling is Ishmael's metaphor for the whole experience of life.

CHAPTER 61: STUBB KILLS A WHALE

Queequeg warns that the great squid is a sure sign that sperm whales are in the vicinity. The next day Ishmael is standing mast-head watch, and, like everyone else on the Pequod on this sultry day, can hardly keep his eyes open. Suddenly a whale blows less than one hundred yards away, and all is commotion on the ship. The boats are quickly lowered. The whale becomes frightened, and suddenly a full-scale chase is under way. Stubb's boat closes in on the whale, and soon Tashtego harpoons it. The whale plows madly ahead, boiling up the sea and blowing furious jets out of his spout, pulling the tiny whaleboat along so fast that its stern rises completely out of the water. The crew pulls the boat up to the whale, and Stubb darts his lance into it time and again. Finally the great animal wallows in exhaustion, and Stubb probes deep with his lance, twisting it until he finds the whale's heart. In its death agony, the creature lashes about violently, blows horrible gore into the air, and then rolls lifeless on the sea.

CHAPTER 62: THE DART

Ishmael wants to explain one point of procedure in the whaleboat. The boat leaves the ship with a whale-killer (a mate, on the Pequod) acting as steersman and the harpooneer pulling the oar nearest the bow. In all the furious activity of racing after the whale, the harpooneer is expected to shout and cheer on his fellow oarsmen, then, at the last minute, jump up and dart the heavy harpoon into the whale. Now, says Ishmael, this is a nonsensical practice. The success of the entire voyage depends upon how well those first darts are made—and yet the system is such that the harpooneer is on the verge of nervous exhaustion when he has to throw the harpoon. Ishmael claims that the headsman should stay at the bow, do no rowing whatsoever, and make both the first dart and the subsequent ones.

COMMENT

Again, Ishmael refers his reflections on whaling to the context of broader experience: "To insure the greatest efficiency in the dart, the harpooneers of this world must start to their feet from out of idleness, and not from out of toil."

CHAPTER 63: THE CROTCH

The crotch is a stick about two feet long, with notches in it to hold the two harpoons attached to the whale line. The second harpoon is carried in hopes of darting it, too, into the whale, so that if one harpoon should pull out in the chase, the other will hold. Ishmael tells us that the second "iron" must be heaved out of the boat, whether into the whale or not, because it might otherwise be flung around and butcher the crew. The danger from the spare harpoons is multiplied when more than one whaleboat gets fast to a single whale. The harpoon is indeed "a dangling, sharp-edged terror" during the chase.

MOBY-DICK
CHAPTERS 64–81

CHAPTER 64: STUBB'S SUPPER

Since there is no wind, the Pequod cannot sail to the floating whale, so the three whale boats fix lines to it and laboriously tow it back to the ship. The task takes several hours, and it is longer after dark when the whale is fastened to the Pequod's side for the night. Stubb, who likes whale steak, exuberantly insists upon having a midnight supper from his victim. At the same time, hundreds of sharks nip at the whale's bulk under the water, tearing out neat blobs of flesh and awakening seamen by slapping their tails against the Pequod's hull below the waterline. Stubb, not hearing the sharks at first, complains that his steak is overcooked.

COMMENT

Ishmael pointedly compares the sharks' feasting on the whale to the sharks' banqueting on human bodies during a sea battle. Humans, he implies, butcher one another as savagely as the mindless sharks feed, by instinct, upon the whale. The analogy is intensified by the fact that Stubb wants his whale steak practically raw—he infers that the sharks know which way whale tastes best.

Stubb orders Fleece, the aged African cook, to preach to the sharks, whose noise begins to disturb him at his meal. Fleece damns the sharks, whereupon Stubb corrects him and tells him to preach a proper sermon. The cook begins: "Belubed fellow-critters"—and goes on to tell them that they must govern their sharkishness, for "all angel is not'ing more dan de shark well goberned." He suggests that the sharks with the biggest mouths should help those with small mouths to a meal, and Stubb responds, "Well done, old Fleece! . . . that's Christianity," and tells Fleece to give the benediction. The cook's "benediction" is "Cussed fellow critters! Kick up de damndest row as ever you can; fill your dam' bellies 'til dey bust—and den die." After this, Stubb tells Fleece that he doesn't know how to cook, makes fun of his religious notions, and gives him special orders for meals the next day. Fleece finally departs, wishing the whale had eaten Stubb rather than the reverse and saying that Stubb is more sharkish than "Massa Shark hisself."

COMMENT

This "sermon" by Fleece is the second of the book, and it contrasts markedly with Father Mapple's in many ways. It is also one of the funniest chapters in the book.

CHAPTER 65: THE WHALE AS A DISH

The whale, Ishmael tell us, has been regarded as a delicacy in many countries. Sixteenth-century Frenchmen and English-men enjoyed it, for instance. But these days only the Eskimos and such case-hardened whalemen as Stubb care for whale steak. The whale makes too large a dish, says Ishmael, and is too rich—and furthermore, many landlubbers have a horror of eating anything from the sea.

COMMENT

Ishmael adds another touch to the theme of cannibal-ism by pointing out that Stubb adds insult to injury by eating the whale by the light of a whale-oil lamp—the whale aids in consuming itself. In Chapter 95, we shall see that the flensers, or blubber-cutters, wear a protec-tive coat of whale's skin, and in Chapter 96, that the fires for melting down the fat are started with scraps of dried blubber. In these cases, too, the whale helps to destroy itself. In Chapter 66, the wounded sharks attack their own bodies. The world follows the principles of self-destructive cannibalism.

CHAPTER 66: THE SHARK MASSACRE

A whale captured late at night is usually lashed to the side of the ship until morning, since the whole crew is needed to cut it to pieces. In the Pacific this method will not do, because the sharks will devour almost the entire carcass of a whale in the course of a night. Here in the Indian Ocean the sharks are not so numerous; nevertheless, to prevent severe damage to Stubb's whale, Queequeg and another crewman are suspended over the Pequod's side on a scaffold, and they slaughter a great many sharks with the whaling-spades. These are broad, razor-sharp blades on the ends of twenty-foot poles. The sharks are so voracious that they not only eat each other, but even tear at their own wounds in a horrifying carnage.

COMMENT

For the third chapter in a row, Melville stresses the theme of cannibalism and voracity in nature. The shark is so vicious that it is even dangerous after death—Queequeg almost loses his hand when he tries to shut the jaw of a dead shark hauled on deck for its skin.

CHAPTER 67: CUTTING IN

The whale is caught on a Saturday night; on Sunday, the gigantic blocks and tackles for stripping blubber are hoisted up the mainmast and the process of peeling the blubber off the whale begins. A hole is cut in the whale's fatty side by the mates and a hook is inserted into the hole. The men heave mightily on the windlass attached to the stripping tackle, and the blubber is slowly peeled off in a long strip (called a "scarf"), much the way an orange is peeled continuously. The whale flops over and over in the water as this ribbon of blubber comes off. When the scarf has been hoisted as high as the blocks and tackles will carry it, a second hook is attached to it near the whale; then a harpooneer hacks the piece off just above the new hook, and while the second scarf is peeled, the first is lowered into a place in the hold called the blubber-room and coiled up for storage.

CHAPTER 68: THE BLANKET

Ishmael tells us that he has given a great deal of thought to the subject of the whale's skin, and has decided that the blubber is its skin, for no other layer can be peeled from the whale's carcass. The blubber ranges from eight to fifteen inches thick, and is of the consistency of beef. We may get some idea of the enormous size of the whale, says Ishmael, from the fact that three-quarters of the "skin" alone of a large whale boils down to enough oil to fill one hundred barrels, approximately ten tons in weight.

All this blubber keeps the whale warm in the icy waters of the polar oceans. The value of this warm outer covering suggests, according to Ishmael, "The rare virtue of thick walls, and the rare virtue of interior spaciousness"—and he recommends that men be "cool at the equator," a piece of advice he considers hard to follow.

CHAPTER 69: THE FUNERAL

After the blubber has been stripped off the carcass, the head is severed from the body and the great hulk is turned loose to float astern. For hours the carcass remains in sight, and the sharks and carnivorous sea birds surround it. If another ship sees the carcass, it will probably mistake it for uncharted rocks or shoals, with the possible result that for years mariners will avoid the area as a dangerous one.

COMMENT

Again, Melville stresses the cannibalism of nature, as Ishmael comments on the vultures and sharks battening on what is left of the whale's corpse.

CHAPTER 70: THE SPHYNX

The whale's head is valuable, so it is secured to the side of the ship. Ishmael marvels at the skill shown by the mate who severs the immense head—one third of the huge whale's bulk—from a body that has no neck. The cutter must reach an invisible point on the spine, through many feet of flesh, often in a rolling sea that covers much of the whale's carcass.

After the whale's head has been secured, about noon, the Pequod's crew go below to dinner, and Ahab comes on deck alone. He stares over the side at the whale's head, and then begins to speak to it. He ponders everything the whale must have seen in its roving life, and the fact that it cannot communicate its knowledge to man. His thoughts are interrupted by the cry: "Sail ho!" Ahab is somewhat cheered by the thought of seeing a ship, and comments that a breeze would improve things still more.

COMMENT

Ahab addresses the whale as if it were a human being. Ahab has spoken of Moby Dick all along as if he had human qualities, and here it is apparent that he extends this belief to all whales. Melville has treated the theme of cannibalism in several previous chapters; this soliloquy further stresses his belief that all living creatures are one.

CHAPTER 71: THE JEROBOAM'S STORY

The strange ship proves to be the Jeroboam of Nantucket. Its captain pulls near to the Pequod in a whale boat but refuses to come aboard, for his ship is suffering from an epidemic. Stubb recognizes one of the men in the captain's boat crew as a Shaker who was described to him earlier by one of the Town-Ho's crew. This madman thinks he is the archangel Gabriel, and his prophecies have so terrified the Jeroboam's ignorant and superstitious crew that he has free run of the ship despite his uselessness as a whaleman.

When Ahab asks the Jeroboam's captain, Mayhew, if he has seen Moby Dick, Mayhew tells Ahab that his first mate, Macey, was knocked overboard a whaleboat by a blow of Moby Dick's tail. Mayhew asks if Ahab will pursue Moby Dick, and Ahab

vows that he will. Gabriel interrupts, warning Ahab to remember Macey's death. Ahab remembers that he has a letter
aboard for one of the Jeroboam's crew. The letter, brought on
deck, turns out to be for none other than the dead mate;
nevertheless, Ahab sends it down to Captain Mayhew on the
end of a cutting spade. But crazy Gabriel gets the letter, im-
pales it on a knife, and throws it up onto the Pequod's deck at
Ahab's feet after screeching "Nay, keep it thyself . . . thou art
soon going that way" (after Macey). With this the boat's crew
ship oars and row away.

COMMENT

This is the third ship the Pequod has encountered,
although the meeting with the Town-Ho was reported
only indirectly. The Goney was unable to communicate
with the Pequod, and the Jeroboam has only bad news
and warnings to offer.

Jeroboam is another of the many biblical names in the
novel. The biblical Jeroboam was a king who refused to
obey God's laws and in consequence died. Gabriel is
the archangel who prophesied the birth of Christ to Mary.
The Shakers are a religious sect that was very strong in
Melville's time; they lived apart from the rest of
society, and their most notable doctrine was their ban
on sexual intercourse.

Once again, Ahab's only concern in contacting another
ship is news of Moby Dick. He has no fear of the illness
aboard the Jeroboam, he barely remembers that he has
mail for one of its officers.

CHAPTER 72: THE MONKEY-ROPE

Ishmael tells us that the blubber hooks were fastened to the
"scarfs" on this particular whale by Queequeg. Fastening the
hooks is a hazardous job, even for the whaling industry, for
the harpooneer must walk the slippery back of the whale,

which is submerged most of the time. To add to Queequeg's danger, circumstances demand that he stay on the whale during the entire "flensing" (stripping) operation. Aboard the Pequod, the practice is to attach the harpooner who does this work to the man who pulls the oar immediately behind him— so Ishmael is linked to Queequeg by means of a line, called a monkey-rope. Ishmael feels that this bond with Queequeg reflects the interdependence of all men; no man can survive without the aid of others. Several times, Ishmael is almost pulled over the side. To add to Queequeg's problems, the sharks continue to attack the whale, and Daggoo and Tashtego continue to butcher them with whaling-spades. Ishmael muses: Queequeg's situation is every man's; "those sharks, your foes; those spades, your friends; and what between sharks and spades you are in a sad pickle and peril, poor lad." When Queequeg returns exhausted to the deck, the steward offers him a cup of ginger and water. Stubb, outraged, demands that the steward produce good whiskey to warm Queequeg, and Starbuck agrees. They throw the ginger, which had been supplied by Aunt Charity, overboard.

COMMENT

Again Ishmael underscores the close bond that exists between Queequeg and himself, even going so far as to say, "we two, for the time, were wedded" As usual, however, Ishmael conceives of his personal experience as analogous to a larger truth.

CHAPTER 73: STUBB AND FLASK KILL A RIGHT WHALE; AND THEN HAVE A TALK OVER HIM

The Pequod enters fields of brit once more, indicating that right whales may be near, and Ahab announces that they will capture a right whale if possible. This comes as a surprise to all, since the right whale is (as Stubb puts it) a "lump of foul lard." A right whale is sighted, two boats are lowered, and after an exciting chase the whale is killed. Flask, in one whaleboat, explains to Stubb, in the other, that Fedallah has convinced Ahab that a ship with a sperm whale's head on the starboard side and a right whale's head on the port can never capsize. Stubb and Flask discuss Fedallah; Stubb asserts that Fedallah is the devil, and that he, Stubb, will heave him overboard if he gets the opportunity. Both are quite concerned about Fedallah's intentions toward Ahab, and Stubb vows to keep an eye on him.

COMMENT

Fedallah's influence upon Ahab is becoming apparent. Stubb says that Fedallah is the devil, and Melville mentions that the Parsee stands in Ahab's shadow, so as to cast none of his own. (The devil, of course, is supposed to have no shadow.)

Ishmael remarks that sailing with two whale's heads dragging it down, the Pequod reminds him of a man who counterbalances Locke's head (Locke, the great English empirical philosopher) with that of Kant (the great German idealist philosopher, radically opposed to Locke) in his view of the world. He is still paralleling his whaling experiences and his general theories of existence—and will continue to do so.

CHAPTER 74: THE SPERM WHALE'S HEAD— CONTRASTED VIEW

Ishmael contrasts the heads of the Pequod's two whales for the reader's benefit. The sperm whale's head is the more symmetrical and shows more character; it has a "pervading dignity." The sperm whale's eye, about the size of a horse's eye, is at the back of the jaw and the ear is immediately behind that. The most remarkable feature of the whale's eyes is that, separated by the gigantic bulk of the head, they cannot possibly present a single, unified impression to the animal's brain; there must be two impressions, one from each eye, delivered to the brain. (This fact, Ishmael thinks, could account for the great confusion shown by some whales when being attacked from more than one side.) The ear is even smaller than the eye, hardly large enough to insert the end of a quill of a pen into it.

If we look into the whale's mouth, we see a glossy white membrane covering the entire surface. The enormous jaw, about fifteen feet long, contains rows of long powerful teeth. Sometimes a sulking whale lets his jaw hang straight down into the water, far below the surface—then, says Ishmael, the jaw is even more terrifying. The jaw is usually hoisted on deck, to have the valuable teeth pulled out with a tackle on the mast; then the jaw itself is sawed into pieces.

COMMENT

Along with Chapters 67 and 68, this chapter gives the reader a number of specific details about the appearance of sperm whales in general and thus about Moby Dick's appearance in particular. Although he has made no appearance in the novel yet, he is the title character and the motivator of all of the action. Melville never lets the reader forget his still-offstage main character. He continues to build up Moby Dick's biography for the reader.

CHAPTER 75: THE RIGHT WHALE'S HEAD— CONTRASTED VIEW

Ishmael crosses the Pequod's deck and looks at the right whale's head. It has none of the elegance of the high-domed sperm whale's head; on the contrary, it looks rather like a gigantic, moccasin-toed shoe. It has spout-holes and a crusty, lumpy green mass (called a "crown") on top, and an enormous lower lip and jaw, which give it a pouting appearance. Inside the mouth is a huge tongue, and a series of vertical slots—which resemble Venetian blinds—for straining out food as it cruises through the water.

CHAPTER 76: THE BATTERING-RAM

Before leaving the sperm whale's head entirely, Ishmael points out that it rises vertically out of the water, and has, to all appearances, no sensitive parts whatsoever. The eyes and ears are twenty or more feet from the forehead, the spout hole is on top, and the long jaw is entirely below the head and well back of the great blank forehead. The forehead is incredibly tough—no harpoon or lance can pierce it. And all this dead mass, which Ishmael compares in toughness to a horse's hoof, is driven by the most powerful living creature in the world.

COMMENT

Melville continually reminds the reader of the immense size and strength of sperm whales in general and thus of Moby Dick in particular. This chapter suggests that the sperm whale is all but invulnerable, further building up the reader's anticipation of an eventual meeting between Ahab and Moby Dick.

CHAPTER 77: THE GREAT HEIDELBURGH TUN

If we divide the sperm whale's head diagonally from lower front to upper rear, we will find the skull of the whale in the lower half and the "case," containing the precious spermaceti oil, in the upper. The case (or "Heidelburgh Tun," as Ishmael calls it, after a famous barrel which held nearly fifty thousand gallons) is as long as the whale's head—perhaps twenty-five feet—and generally holds about five hundred gallons. It is broken into from the "neck."

CHAPTER 78: CISTERN AND BUCKETS

Tashtego, Stubb's harpooneer, climbs the mainmast and goes out on the yard-arm (the horizontal spar on the mast) over the whale's head. There he rigs up a pulley and rope, with a bucket attached, for scooping the spermaceti out of the head. Tashtego cuts into the case with extreme care, and the process of transferring the precious stuff begins. Toward the end of the job Tashtego slips and falls head first into the oozy case, now twenty feet deep! As Daggoo hurries to help him, the whale's head tears loose from one of the two giant hooks that have held it fast against the Pequod. The colossal head swings crazily over the sea for a moment, then slips free and sinks. Instantly Queequeg, with a sword in his hand, is over the side of the ship and rescues Tashtego.

COMMENT

This is the second time Queequeg has saved a man from drowning. The episode further emphasizes the dangers in attacking whales: Even dead, the whale can still kill a man.

CHAPTER 79: THE PRAIRIE

Ishmael reflects upon the enormous wrinkled blank wall of the whale's forehead. Of all the impressive high foreheads known to man, the whale's is by far the largest, with the grandest wrinkles. Ishmael sees a "high and mighty god-like dignity" in the whale's forehead, as well as a vast mystery. To look at the whale's face is to see no expression or meaning whatsoever.

COMMENT

As Ahab did in Chapter 70, Ishmael tries to "read the riddle" of the whale's brow. But like the vast face of nature, the whale's forehead is inscrutable; whatever mysteries it may hide, Ishmael admits he cannot grasp them.

CHAPTER 80: THE NUT

In a full-grown whale, Ishmael says, the skull will be at least twenty feet long. Regarded from the rear, the whale's skull looks like a human skull seen from the same angle. Toward the rear of the skull is a hollow of less than a cubic foot; in this recess the whale's brain is located. Considering the whale's bulk, the brain is small indeed by comparison—but Ishmael defends the whale by saying that its spinal column is as big around as its brain, and that he judges a man's character by his backbone, not his brain. The whale's appearance is deceptive, says Ishmael—the whale, "like all things that are mighty, wears a false brow to the common world."

CHAPTER 81: THE PEQUOD MEETS THE VIRGIN

As the Pequod sails onward it encounters a German vessel, the Jungfrau, or Virgin. Ishmael tells us that German ships rarely sail to the Pacific, although at one time Germans were among the leading whalers of the world. The Jungfrau's captain lowers a boat and hastens toward the Pequod, swinging in his hand an odd object that proves to be an oil can. Here is a whaler without oil enough to light a lantern! Ahab asks for news of Moby Dick, but Captain de Deer has none. Aboard Ahab's ship he gets the can filled and departs quickly, but before he can get back to the Jungfrau, whales are sighted.

Boats are lowered from both ships, with the Jungfrau's well in the lead. Rowing mightily, the Pequod's boats pass all the others except that of the German captain, who thanklessly throws his oil can and other equipment at them. Infuriated, the crews redouble their efforts and close in on the other whaleboat. At the last moment, all three of the Pequod's harpooneers dart their weapons over the head of the German captain; all three find the mark in the pitiful, maimed old whale that is their target. The old whale runs briefly, then he dives. For several ticklish minutes the three whaleboats stand almost perpendicular in the water under the strain of the great whale's weight, then the whale rises close to the boats. Dart after dart of the lances pierce the whale, who is blind as well as crippled. Then Flask sees a horrible growth on its side, which he promptly stabs. The whale spouts blood in agony, and then rolls over and dies.

The three boats tow the hulk back to the ship, but after it is chained to the side it begins to sink, causing the Pequod to list alarmingly. Finally it becomes necessary to hack through one of the chains; the weight of the whale snaps the others, and the great corpse sinks like lead into the sea. Shortly thereafter, the Germans are seen ignorantly chasing finback whales, a species too fast to be captured.

COMMENT

Like many of the other names in the novel, the Virgin's name is symbolic. Just as a virgin is ignorant of the mysteries of sex and motherhood, the Virgin in the novel is ignorant of the mystery of Moby Dick.

This chapter reveals a new aspect of Flask's personality; he is needlessly cruel. The old whale had no chance against the harpooners and would have succumbed in any case; Flask's puncturing the abcess in the whale's side caused it to die in great agony. Starbuck tries to stop him, but is not in time.

MOBY-DICK
CHAPTERS 82–101

CHAPTER 82: THE HONOR
AND GLORY OF WHALING

Ishmael tells us that he has become convinced that whaling is an ancient activity, as well as an exalted one. The first whaleman was the Greek hero Perseus, who killed a sea monster to save Andromeda, a princess. The skeleton of this monster, Ishmael contends, was preserved in a temple of Joppa—the city from which the second great whaleman, Jonah, began his voyage. A third great whaleman was St. George. His monster could hardly have been a mere "crawling reptile of the land," says Ishmael: "Any man may kill a snake, but only a Perseus, a St. George . . . have the heart in them to march boldly up to a whale." A fourth whaleman of great renown was Hercules, who, like Jonah, was swallowed by a whale and then coughed up again. Fifth on Ishmael's list is Vishnoo, one of the three persons of the Hindu godhead: Vishnoo became incarnate in a whale. These five—Perseus, St. George, Jonah, Hercules, and Vishnoo—constitute a very special enrollment for the whaleman's club.

COMMENT

Again, Ishmael stresses the importance of whaling to different countries and different times. The inclusion of St. George is questionable, since the creature in the legend is invariably a dragon, not any kind of sea monster.

CHAPTER 83: JONAH HISTORICALLY REGARDED

Ishmael mentions that some Nantucket whalemen doubt the truth of the story of Jonah and the whale. For various reasons they doubt that a man could survive in a whale's belly; further, one old man whom Ishmael calls Sag-Harbor cannot accept that the whale could have travelled from the Mediterranean Sea to Nineveh (where Jonah was delivered up) in only three days.

COMMENT

Ishmael seems to feel that old Sag-Harbor should not disbelieve the story of Jonah on literal grounds, but that he should accept it as a miracle. For Ishmael, faith is not a matter of subjecting the Bible to literal analysis, but accepting and appreciating the miracles that occur.

CHAPTER 84: PITCHPOLING

Shortly after the meeting with the Jungfrau, the Pequod raises a school of whales, which flee from it rapidly. The boats pursue, and Stubb's boat gets fast to a whale. But the whale, instead of diving, continues to swim rapidly on the surface. Since the great strain this causes will inevitably wrench the harpoon out of the whale's flesh, Stubb resorts to pitchpoling to weaken the whale. The pitchpole is a lance like the harpoon, but much longer and lighter; it is balanced in the hand and thrown in a long arc at the whale's vitals, then pulled back by means of the rope to which it is attached. Stubb flings the pitchpole into the whale again and again from the wildly careening boat, until the whale goes into his death-flurry.

CHAPTER 85: THE FOUNTAIN

For thousands of years, says Ishmael, whales have been spouting in seas all over the world, but even yet no one knows exactly what the spout is. That the whale breathes through his spout is quite certain, but what about the nature of the spout itself? Is it air, or water, or both? Although many whalemen think the spout is poisonous, Ishmael thinks it is simply an acrid mist, which it is well to stay away from because it stings.

COMMENT

In this chapter, Melville explains a characteristic of whales that makes them vulnerable and is the key to the whaling industry. Because the whale is a mammal, it needs to breathe; therefore, it needs to surface periodically. A whale can inhale an hour's worth of air in one trip to the surface. If its breathing is disturbed by whalers, it will sound, but will return to the surface shortly in an attempt to inhale the full quantity of air it needs. If the whaler can interrupt the spouting, he forces the whale to surface and become vulnerable to attack. The whaleman tries to time the whale. This is one of the few points of vulnerability about Ahab's otherwise formidable object of revenge, Moby Dick.

CHAPTER 86: THE TAIL

Parodying nature poets who sing the praises of animals, Ishmael tells us that he will now praise the whale's tail. It is a thing of tremendous power and grace, more than twenty feet broad in the full-grown sperm whale. Its colossal strength is increased, in Ishmael's opinion, by the fact that it is composed of three layers, with the fibers of the middle layer running crosswise to the fibers of the two outer ones. Ishmael argues that in the whale's tail, as in all things, "strength never impairs harmony or beauty." The whale does five things with its tail: swims by folding the tail under its body, then forcing it to the rear; swings the tail as a weapon against whaleboats; feels in the water for food—and for enemies—with the tail; plays with it by slapping it down on the water with a crack that can be heard for miles; and flips it high in the air when it is about to sound, or dive. The whale's tail, Ishmael implies, is almost as much a marvel and mystery as is its head.

COMMENT

Again, Melville uses the device of general, nonfiction-style description to tell the reader some very specific details about Moby Dick. Moby Dick was accused earlier of knocking the Jeroboam's first mate, Macey, overboard with a blow of his tail. This chapter tells the reader exactly how powerful a weapon this tail is: how big it is, what it looks like, how it is constructed, and what else a whale uses it for.

CHAPTER 87: THE GRAND ARMADA

The Pequod sails through a passage in the Malay peninsula, called the Straits of Sunda, heading for the China Sea. On the way through the narrow straits the mast-head watches send up a cry; an enormous school of whales two or three miles wide is sighted. The Pequod crowds on all sails, and as it chases the "Grand Armada" of whales, a Malay pirate ship is sighted in the wake. The Pequod sails out of the straits into the Pacific, outdistancing the pirates, but getting no closer to the whales. The boats are lowered and the crews give chase until they are about to give up, when suddenly the school of whales stops, and begins to mill around in confusion.

The boats fan out and close in on the whales, each attacking a lone whale on the circumference of the pack. The whale that Queequeg harpoons drags Starbuck's boat (in which Ishmael is bow oarsman) into the very heart of the school, between the heaving bulks of countless whales. The whalemen shout jovial commands to the whales as they scrape by. Starbuck also strikes three other whales with harpoons that have druggs (big wooden buoys that will drag behind the stricken whales and tire them out) attached to them. In the center of this immense school of whales, all is calm, and the sailors get a fantastic view of the ordinary life of the whale. They see mothers nursing their calves, and even one newborn calf still attached to the mother by the umbilical cord. Fathoms down, whales float calmly on their sides, eyeing Starbuck's boat. Others come up to the boat like pets; Queequeg pats some on their foreheads and Starbuck scratches their backs with his lance.

This peaceful scene is violently disrupted by a severely wounded whale, which has broken loose from a whaleboat and, by some freak accident, carried off a cutting-spade entangled in the harpoon line. In its agony this creature flails its tail about, hacking many other whales with the cutting-spade. This horrible event stirs the great herd, and hundreds of them begin to crowd into the center. Rowing and steering frantically, the boatmen scramble beside, between, and over dozen of whales, Queequeg prods gigantic sides with his harpoon, and oars scrape many a whale's back, as the boat barely escapes. The Pequod captures just one whale out of all these hundreds, or thousands, of leviathans.

COMMENT

This is the first indication in the novel that men and whales need not be enemies. The sequence of the boats rowing with the herd, and the herd behaving like pet dogs, is charming and beautiful. It is a strong contrast to the novel's many other scenes of encounters between whales and men.

CHAPTER 88: SCHOOLS AND SCHOOLMASTERS

The immense school of whales encountered in the last chapter was rather unusual. Generally, Ishmael tells us, the schools are smaller, ranging from twenty to fifty in number. These smaller schools are of two kinds: one made up almost entirely of females; the other composed of energetic young males. The schools of females are always attended by one full-grown male, who acts as both husband and guardian to his harem. This whale vigorously drives away any other males that approach the herd—and, Ishmael points out, frequently bears the scars of violent combat with other bulls (males). The whaleman usually avoids these harem-keepers if other game is in sight, because they are inclined to be extremely pugnacious toward whaleboats. When they grow old they leave their harems and take up a solitary life.

The herds of young bulls ("forty-barrel-bulls," Ishmael calls them) are rollicking and reckless ("like a mob of young collegians"), and are more dangerous to encounter than most whales. (The most dangerous of all are "those wondrous gray-headed, grizzled whales, sometimes met, and these will fight you like grim fiends." Moby Dick is such a whale.)

COMMENT

This chaper gives the reader an idea of the ordinary social life of a whale like Moby Dick.

CHAPTER 89: FAST-FISH AND LOOSE-FISH

Ishmael now explains an aspect of whaling he has not yet touched upon. Sometimes a whale that has been harpooned escapes from the boat that was fast to it, only to be recaptured and killed by another. Ishmael explains that the whalers have two universally accepted, unwritten laws to cover this situation. "A Fast-Fish belongs to the party fast to it." "A Loose-Fish is fair game for anybody who can soonest catch it." Ironically, the conciseness of these laws has given rise to many lawsuits and arguments over their precise interpretation. Laws of possession all over the world share this same ambiguity.

COMMENT

Melville implies that kings, politicians, landlords, moneylenders, churches, and nations all apply the laws of fast-fish and loose-fish for their own selfish purposes. Greed is universal among men.

CHAPTER 90: HEADS OR TAILS

Ishmael extends the protest of the preceding chapter by giving an example of the injustice perpetuated upon the helpless by the powerful. A certain English law makes the whale a "royal fish," giving the King and Queen the absolute possession of any whale captured on the English coast. After much difficulty a group of English seamen captured and beached a whale, which was immediately claimed by a certain duke, who was granted his "right" to the whale by the King. Despite the logical, and desperate, pleas of the whalers, the official simply replied mechanically, over and over again. "It is his." A clergyman interceded for the seamen, but was told by the duke to mind his own business. Ishmael finds this law preposterous. Perhaps, he hints, there is a resemblance between the heads of kings and the heads of royal fish which makes the king's claim logical.

COMMENT

Ishmael shows his sympathies for the downtrodden, using ridicule, irony, and sarcasm to make his opinion clear.

CHAPTER 91: THE PEQUOD MEETS THE ROSE-BUD

Once more the Pequod settles into an uneventful routine, sailing over a calm sea. One quiet day, however, an unpleasant odor warns the crew that the ship is approaching a dead whale on the sea. As the stench grows, a French whaler is sighted with a couple of blasted whales (whales that have died uncaptured on the sea) fastened to its sides. The practical Stubb immediately suspects that one of the whales may contain a cache of ambergris (see Chapter 92), and immediately begins to plot to get it. He approaches the foul-smelling Bouton-de-Rose (Rose-bud) and asks if anyone has seen Moby Dick. One man aboard speaks English; he replies that he has never heard of such a thing as a white whale.

Stubb sees that the Rose-bud's crew doesn't relish cutting up the two stinking whales, and he and the Englishman (who is first mate of the ship) combine to get the crew out of "this dirty scrape" of a job. Stubb will speak to the French captain, and the Englishman will translate his words, telling the captain the whales are diseased and will infect everyone aboard. Stubb takes the opportunity to insult the captain at length, but the Englishman "translates" his words as he and Stubb had agreed. The captain orders the whales cut loose, and Stubb tows one of them away. When he is hidden from the Frenchman by the Pequod's hull, Stubb cuts into his whale and comes out with several handfuls of ambergris, worth, at the time, a gold guinea (one English pound) per ounce.

COMMENT

Like the Virgin, the Rose-bud has no knowledge of Moby Dick. The similarity between the two ships' names is no accident. It is ironic that the foul-smelling ship has a sweet-smelling name.

Stubb's practical and callous sense of humor is the center of this chapter. He schemes to insult the French captain with impunity, and to rob the crew of the precious ambergris. He succeeds entirely, and the matter does not trouble his conscience.

CHAPTER 92: AMBERGRIS

Ambergris, we are told, is a yellow-gray, waxy substance found in sick whales; the name comes from two French words meaning gray amber (though amber and ambergris have nothing in common). It is valued for its spicy fragrance and flavor, and is used as a spice in cooking and in the manufacture of perfumes, candles, and hair-oil.

Ishmael takes the opportunity, while discoursing on odors, to defend the whalemen against the charge that whaling is a smelly industry. It is only the northern whalers, who preserve the blubber whole and then boil it in port, that stink. The southern whalemen "try out" (boil down) the blubber immediately after the whale is killed, while it is still fresh and sweet.

COMMENT

This chapter is noteworthy for its use of paradoxes. The sweetness of all substances, ambergris, is found in the midst of the most loathsome decay. It is named after a substance that bears almost no resemblance to it, and used by ladies who would be horrified by its original source. To describe the odor of the northern whalers, Ishmael uses the metaphor of excavating in a graveyard (where life ends) for the foundation for a maternity hospital (where life begins).

CHAPTER 93: THE CASTAWAY

Pip, the Caribbean boy who was introduced in Chapter 40, has never gone out in the whaleboats. However, when a member of Stubbs' whaleboat crew is injured, Pip is chosen to replace him. On Pip's second trip in the whaleboat, a harpooned whale gives the boat a mighty rap with his tail right under Pip's seat. The terrified Pip leaps from the boat and is caught in the whale line, while at the same moment the whale starts his run—the fouled line will strangle Pip in a matter of seconds. Stubb orders the line cut; Pip is saved, the whale is lost. Half scolding, half humorously, Stubb warns Pip that if he jumps again he will be left behind.

Subsequently, in another collision with a whale, Pip is again frightened and again jumps. Stubb leaves him in the sea, thinking that one of the two following whaleboats will pick him up. But the other two boats, not seeing Pip, sight whales and chase them; Pip is left alone in the ocean. Several hours later the Pequod itself, by sheer chance, rescues him, but by this time Pip has gone mad from fear.

COMMENT

Stubb's command that the line be cut to save Pip shows that he is not completely heartless. However, his lack of imagination prevents him from understanding Pip's terror at being abandoned in the ocean. Had Pip been in the boat of the more sensitive Starbuck, he would almost certainly have been rescued immediately. Although the chance of the other boats' not having seen Pip plays a part in his fate, Stubb is largely responsible for the boy's breakdown.

Ishmael is sympathetic to Pip's tragedy. While the rest of the crew calls Pip an idiot, Ishmael believes that Pip is much closer to God than the rest of them, and comments that "man's insanity is heaven's sense."

CHAPTER 94: A SQUEEZE OF THE HAND

Stubb's whale is brought alongside the Pequod, and the long process of extracting the oil is begun. As the blubber is stripped off, it is placed into large tubs. Since it must be kept soft before going to the try-works, several men, including Ishmael, knead it continually. After the exertion of chasing the whales, this job, done under a tranquil sky, is so relaxing that Ishmael finds himself daydreaming. He imagines himself exhorting all his fellow workers to cherish the highest ideals of friendliness, and wishes he could always feel the contentment he experiences while "squeezing case."

Ishmael also describes several other parts of the whale—whitehorse, plum-pudding, slobgollion, curry, and nippers. Then he glances at the blubber-room, where two men are at work—one hooking pieces of blubber, the other chopping those pieces into chunks small enough to be carried. The chopping is done in bare feet and the loss of a toe is a common accident.

COMMENT

In this chapter and several that follow, Ishmael fills us in on the actual details of the trying-out process, whereby the whale oil is produced. These chapters explain in detail the relationship between whales and human beings from the human point of view: They tell exactly how the whale is dismembered and what all the parts are used for.

CHAPTER 95: THE CASSOCK

Before the pieces of blubber are boiled, they are cut into slices (so thin that they are called "Bible leaves") by a seaman whose title is "mincer." The mincer first garbs himself in the skin stripped from a conical section of the whale's anatomy. The skin is stripped off in one piece, turned inside out, and dried; then arm holes are cut into it. Thus dressed, he reminds Ishmael of a kind of priest or minister with a special ritual to perform.

COMMENT

This chapter suggests cannibalism. A man dressed in a whale's skin cuts up a whale; the whale helps to destroy itself.

CHAPTER 96: THE TRY-WORKS

The try-works are a brick kiln about eight feet long, ten feet wide, and five feet high, located between the foremast and mainmast. Two great metal pots are set into it, and under them are two furnaces. The top is covered by a hatch when the works are not in use, as is the front entrance to the furnaces. The try-works are started on this voyage late in the evening, and are burning fiercely by midnight. Both the flames and the smell of the smoke remind Ishmael of hell as he watches, fascinated, from the helm. The weird flickering of the fire and the red-lit shapes of the harpooners laboring at the works, the sweaty faces of the night-watch and the wild laughter of the men as they spin yarns to each other seem infernal—even the ship itself, with a crew of pagans and savages, strikes Ishmael's imagination as "the material counterpart of her monomaniac commander's soul."

For hours Ishmael stands at the tiller (the jawbone of a whale), when, suddenly, he awakens from a brief doze and becomes "horribly conscious of something fatally wrong." To his amazement he realizes that the fire has, as it were, hypnotized him; he is facing over the stern of the ship. He recovers just in time to prevent the ship from capsizing. Ishmael learns a lesson from this experience—not to look too long into the face of fire.

CHAPTER 97: THE LAMP

Ishmael tells us that in a whaler, unlike a merchant ship, all is well illuminated below decks. On a merchantman oil is very scarce, but on a whaler, of course, it is superabundant.

COMMENT

Again, the whale helps to destroy itself. The whalemen work on the whale's carcass by the light of whale-oil lamps.

CHAPTER 98: STOWING DOWN AND CLEARING UP

After the oil has been boiled it is poured, still hot, into great

six-barrel casks. The casks are wrestled about the deck, sometimes in a heavy sea, until they are sealed thoroughly. When
the oil has cooled, the hatchways are opened and the casks
are stored below decks. Then the whalemen clean the decks,
using a lye made from the whale's ashes. A day or two after
the trying-out of blubber, Ishmael says, no one could guess
that a whale had been butchered on the deck. But at any
moment the sighting of another whale may start the whole
backbreaking cycle once more. Life is the same, in Ishmael's
opinion: As soon as we think we have achieved something
significant, another ideal presents itself, "and away we sail to
fight some other world."

CHAPTER 99: THE DOUBLOON

Ahab has the habit of pacing the quarter-deck. One morning
while stumping about the deck, he stops to look at the doubloon, which he fastened to the mainmast as reward for the
first man to sight Moby Dick. The coin is from Ecuador; it has
an inscription around its border; three mountain peaks and
the sun above them with a flame coming from one, a tower
on the second, and a crowing cock on the third; and over all
are ranged the signs of the zodiac. Ahab sees the images on
the coin as symbols of his own stregth and his suffering.
Starbuck looks at the coin and sees the three mountains as
the Trinity, and the sun as a symbol of benevolent righteous-
ness. However, he is saddened, remembering that at night the
encouraging sun is never visible.

Next Stubb comes past, looks at the coin in his turn, and
thinks first of its worth as a piece of money he would like to
spend. However, curiosity overcomes him as he continues to
look at the images, and he reads and interprets the cycle of
the twelve signs of the zodiac. He sees Flask coming and
hides so that he will overhear what Flask thinks of the coin.
One at a time, several others follow Flask, and Stubb listens to
all and comments on their views of the doubloon.

Flask sees only sixteen dollars, which will buy nine hundred and sixty cigars. The old Manxman (introduced in Chapter 40) sees a warning of a meeting with the White Whale. Queequeg compares the doubloon's markings to his own tattoos. Fedallah bows to the gold piece, causing Stubb to label him a fire-worshipper (a devil). Pip gazes at the doubloon and repeats three times, "I look, you look, he looks; we look, ye look, they look." Dismissing Pip's speeches as crazy, Stubb leaves. Pip continues to look at the doubloon, calling it the ship's navel, and brokenly predicts that Moby Dick will "nail" Ahab.

COMMENT

Each character in this chapter sees something different in the doubloon, and what each sees illuminates his character for the reader. Ahab concentrates on himself. Starbuck sees religious symbols in which he can take no comfort. Stubb and Flask see only the money. Queequeg is curious about the images and tries to discover what they have in common with those on his body.

Once again, the narrative voice has shifted. The omniscient third-person narrator begins the chapter, continuing through Stubb's soliloquy. From this point on, the chapter consists entirely of dialogue, various characters' soliloquies alternating with Stubb's reactions. Melville draws the reader directly into the scene, presenting the speeches with no narrative comment at all. It is as if the reader, like Stubb, were hiding behind a mast, watching and listening.

CHAPTER 100: LEG AND ARM—THE PEQUOD, OF NANTUCKET, MEETS THE SAMUEL ENDERBY, OF LONDON

The Pequod meets an English ship called the Samuel Enderby. Ahab hails it, asking if its captain has seen the White Whale;

in response the captain raises one arm—like Ahab's leg, it is made of whalebone. Ahab boards the Enderby, where he and Captain Boomer cross ivory limbs in greeting. Then Boomer tells the story of how Moby Dick took off his arm.

The Enderby's boats attacked a small group of whales near the equator, and Boomer's boat harpooned one of them, which swam in wild circles. Suddenly a gigantic white whale breached near them (Ahab recognizes the description of Moby Dick) and bit the line in half. The line got caught in his teeth, so that when the whaleboat pulled up on the line, instead of hauling up on the harpooned whale, it bounced squarely down onto the hump of the infuriated Moby Dick. Boomer jumped into his mate's boat and harpooned Moby Dick, but the great whale smashed the little boat to pieces, scattering the men into the sea and forcing Boomer to cling to the harpoon he had just darted. Moby Dick dove, and the second harpoon tore into Boomer's arm, carrying him down. Luckily the harpoon ripped out, and the Englishman floated to the surface and was rescued. However, his wound was serious, and the arm was eventually amputated by the ship's doctor, Bunger, who is present and is introduced to Ahab. Ahab asks whether the Enderby met Moby Dick again, and Boomer replies that he has seen him twice since, but has left him alone, not wishing to risk further injury. Ahab excitedly asks which way Moby Dick was last heading, and Bunger, realizing that Ahab is in a fever over the white whale, offers to treat him. Ahab violently slams him against the bulwarks and returns to the Pequod to pursue Moby Dick.

COMMENT

Apart from a brief appearance or two, Ahab has been absent from the novel since Chapter 71. Here, Melville places Ahab and his quest back in the center of the action.

Boomer provides a strong contrast to Ahab. Like Ahab,

he has lost a limb to the whale in direct combat, but he bears Moby Dick no grudge; instead, he is thankful that his injury was not more serious, and that he is still able to command his ship. His reaction embodies common sense: He has fought Moby Dick, has been beaten, and acknowledges that Moby Dick is too strong for him.

Boomer warns Ahab against pursuing Moby Dick, saying that it is best to leave him alone, but Ahab ignores the warning. So far, none of the ships the Pequod has met has encouraged Ahab's quest.

CHAPTER 101: THE DECANTER

Ishmael informs us that the Enderby was named after the founder of the most famous whaling firm in England. Samuel Enderby was the first man to equip a whaler to cruise in the South Pacific. Long after the voyage of the Pequod, Ishmael boarded the Enderby, and found her to be a well-equipped and hospitable ship. The English whalers, following a tradition established by the Dutch a couple of centuries earlier, live very well indeed. Their ships are well stocked with solid food and good drink; indeed, when Ishmael boarded the Enderby for a gam, the entire crew got drunk and had to climb the masts, still "top-heavy," to take in sail when a squall blew up.

COMMENT

This chapter furthers the contrast between the cheerful atmosphere on board the Enderby and the savage moods Ahab inflicts upon the Pequod. Boomer's sensible reaction to his battle with Moby Dick has not embittered him, and his ship is a happy place; Ahab has no other thought but vengeance on Moby Dick, and his ship is uneasy, full of secrets, stowaways, and even madness.

MOBY-DICK
CHAPTERS 102–118

CHAPTER 102: A BOWER IN THE ARSACIDES

Now, Ishmael tells us, he will introduce us to the mysteries of the whale's interior, especially his bones. He became familiar with the whale's interior when he saw a whale's skeleton that natives of the Arsacides Islands in the South Pacific had converted into a temple. The skeleton was overgrown and entwined by the lush tropical vegetation. The islanders built an altar within this shady bower, with a flame that escaped through the space where the spout-hole would be. The jawbone of the skeleton was suspended so as to swing back and forth over the worshippers. When Ishmael wanted to measure the skeleton, the priests were furious at his irreverence toward their god. However, he completed his measurements while the priests argued among themselves.

COMMENT

Melville again sounds the Jonah motif of humanity in the jaws of the whale. This motif was introduced in the early chapters of the book, most fully in Father Mapple's sermon. The Spouter-Inn had a bar made of a whale's jaw (and a bartender called Jonah), and the tiller of the Pequod is also made of a whale's jaw.

CHAPTER 103: MEASUREMENT OF THE WHALE'S SKELETON

Ishmael estimates that the weight of a large full-grown sperm whale equals that of eleven hundred men. The skeleton that he measured on the island was seventy-two feet long, which means that the whale itself was about ninety feet long. It had ten ribs on each side, ranging from five to eight feet long, a skull twenty feet long, and forty vertebrae ranging in size from over three feet square to the size of a billiard ball. The ribs of a whale this size are so large that they can be used as beams for bridges over small streams. The skeleton itself reminds Ishmael of the partly finished frame of a large ship.

CHAPTER 104: THE FOSSIL WHALE

Ishmael expounds on the magnitude of the whale as a theme, and then discusses the fossil traces of the ancestors of present-day whales. He tells us that fossils or bones of whale-like creature have been found in France, Italy, England, Scotland, and the United States, including one complete whale's skeleton on a plantation in Alabama. When Ishmael contemplates how far back in time these remains go, he imagines himself transported to a time before written history, when there was little or no habitable land, and the whale was the king of the whole earth. Man seems a newcomer compared to the whale, who has been exploring the seas since the beginning of time.

CHAPTER 105: DOES THE WHALE'S MAGNITUDE DIMINISH?—WILL HE PERISH?

Ishmael wonders whether the whale's size has diminished over the ages, or whether he is liable to extinction. All the trustworthy evidence from fossils indicates that the whale of today is larger, not smaller, than his prehistoric counterpart. The ancient stories of whales measuring up to eight hundred feet are pure myth, as any whaleman can tell you. As far as the problem of the whale's being killed off is concerned, Ishmael has no fears. True, hundreds of thousands of buffalo have been slaughtered in recent years—but the whale lives deep in the sea, not on land. In the time forty whalemen can kill forty whales, forty hunters can kill forty thousand buffalo. It is true that whales are sighted less frequently than in years gone by—but this is because the whales tend more and more to travel in gigantic schools like the "Grand Armada" rather than in small pods. Finally, the whale can retreat to two impregnable fortresses—the north and south polar seas, where the ice floes will forever protect them from pursuit by whalers. Ishmael concludes that individual whales will die, but the species will not.

COMMENT

Ishmael has written four chapters about the thoughts the whale's skeleton has inspired. Although his tone is humorous throughout them, he turns solemn in a number of sentences. Melville uses these chapters to underline the splendor and magnificence of the whale, even in death, even as a skeleton. The description of the Arascidean temple in Chapter 102, the comparisons between the whale and monumental works of architecture in Chapter 103, and the assurance of the whale's immortality in Chapter 105 all inspire the reader with awe.

These four chapters are about sperm whales in general, but again the reader recalls that Moby Dick is a sperm whale, and all four chapters give further details and impressions of Moby Dick.

CHAPTER 106: AHAB'S LEG

In his angry haste to depart from the Samuel Enderby, Ahab twisted and cracked his ivory leg, and he decides to have a new one made. Before the Pequod left Nantucket, Ahab was found unconscious one might, severely hurt by the splintered ivory leg, which had broken mysteriously and almost impaled him. Ahab believed this accident was a direct result of the fact that he was already suffering from the original loss of the leg; misery begets misery as happiness begets happiness. Ahab will take no chances while hunting Moby Dick—he calls the carpenter and the blacksmith. The carpenter is to make him a new leg, using ivory from the whales killed on the voyage, and the blacksmith is to forge the necessary hardware that will allow Ahab to move and control the leg.

COMMENT

Note that Ahab does not blame his accident on Moby Dick, as might have been expected. Instead, he feels that he is doomed to misery, and cannot escape it.

CHAPTER 107: THE CARPENTER

The Pequod's carpenter, like all ship's carpenters, takes care of a variety of mechanical matters on board. He paints oars, pulls teeth, and doctors the crew's minor ailments, besides building anything that is required. He is stolid and impersonal, but has a rusty sense of humor and some wit. Ishmael sums him up by comparing him to a many-bladed pocket-knife: useful for a variety of tasks, but mechanical. The carpenter soliloquizes constantly, but only to keep himself awake.

CHAPTER 108: AHAB AND THE CARPENTER

The carpenter stands by his workbench, chattering to himself and sneezing as the dust from the dry bone that he is filing for Ahab's leg chokes him. He wishes that he had more time to turn out a better product. Ahab approaches to see how the work is progressing. He tells the carpenter that he and the blacksmith should make not one leg but a complete man—a giant fifty feet high with a brass head, a large brain, no heart, and no eyes, only "a skylight on top of his head to illuminate inwards." The carpenter is bewildered, but responds politely.

Ahab then tells the carpenter that he can still feel his original leg, despite its having been amputated. The carpenter is interested; he has heard of such things. Ahab suggests that what he can feel may still be there; that even when one is alone, one cannot be sure that no one else is there. The carpenter cannot follow this idea, and Ahab abruptly asks when the leg will be finished, and leaves the carpenter to it. Ahab cries out passionately at the irony of himself, "proud as a Greek god," depending on a fool like the carpenter for a leg. The carpenter decides that Ahab is a little crazy, and dismisses him from his thoughts as he concentrates on finishing the leg.

COMMENT

Melville returns to a direct, dramatic presentation in this chapter. It opens with stage directions that set the scene, and continues with dialogue only. There is no narrative voice present. The reader is invited into the scene as an eavesdropper. This technique gives Ahab's comment "In thy most solitary hours, then, dost thou not fear eavesdroppers?" an extra level of irony.

This direct presentation of the carpenter bears out Ishmael's comments in the previous chapter. He does soliloquize constantly, but, unlike Ahab, he thinks only about practical matters, like the beautiful leg he might have made if he had had more time.

CHAPTER 109: AHAB AND STARBUCK IN THE CABIN

One morning Starbuck comes into Ahab's cabin to report a serious leak in the whale-oil casks in the hold, and to request permission to "up Burtons and break out" (unload, check, and repair the casks). Ahab is working on his charts, tracing Moby Dick's regular routes, and is irritated at being disturbed. He tells Starbuck that he will not give the order to salvage the oil, and orders him out of the cabin. Starbuck will not go, however; he is respectful, but he insists that Ahab must listen to reason. Ahab is furious at this implied criticism, and orders him out again. Starbuck pleads for an understanding between them, but Ahab insists on his rights as commander of the ship. The two men lock eyes, and Starbuck accepts defeat. He leaves, warning Ahab to beware of himself. Ahab is struck by this idea, and, thinking things over, goes on deck, apologizes to Starbuck, and gives the order to up Burtons and break out.

COMMENT

This chapter is the first serious open conflict between two of the novel's protagonists, and is highly dramatic. It is especially strong because of its contrast in mood to the preceding several chapters, which were uneventful and on the whole rather placid.

Starbuck has been uneasy aboard the Pequod since Ahab first shared with the crew his vow of revenge on Moby Dick. Finally, he openly defies Ahab. Short of mutiny, he cannot refuse to obey Ahab's order, but he protests as strongly as he can. He does not limit his plea to the practical matter of the loss of whale oil, as Stubb or Flask would have done; he reaches out directly to Ahab, man to man, with a plea for mutual understanding. He is concerned for the whole ship, for the crew, and for the material success of the voyage, but he is also concerned for Ahab's spiritual welfare.

CHAPTER 110: QUEEQUEG IN HIS COFFIN

Queequeg is among those who have to work in the slimy blackness of the hold, moving the oil casks to check for leaks. In the cold below decks he catches a chill that leads to a terrible fever, and in a few days he is on the verge of death. He makes an unusual request: He wants to be buried at sea in the kind of canoe-coffin which is supposed to be used for whalemen who die in Nantucket. Accordingly the carpenter is called; he takes measurements and quickly makes a serviceable coffin, which he carries forward to Queequeg for his inspection, despite protests from the crew. Queequeg has himself lifted into it, and finds it suitable. As he lies in state, Pip comes up to him, and asks him a favor. If Queequeg's canoe floats to the Antilles, he should look for Pip and comfort him; Pip has been missing a long time. Starbuck overhears, and pities Pip's lunacy. After this episode, Queequeg regains his health rapidly. When asked the secret of his marvelous recovery, Queequeg simply says that he has some unfinished business ashore (he thinks that a man's death is subject to his own will, except for death caused by natural forces, such as whales). Thereafter, he spends much of his spare time decorating the coffin with designs like the ones tattooed on his body.

COMMENT

Pip no longer knows who he is. Although he remembers his history, he no longer connects his physical body with those memories. He thinks Pip has disappeared and that he must be someone else.

As soon as Queequeg lies down in his coffin, he begins to recover from what everyone thought was a fatal illness. The coffin appears to have healing powers. Remember that it was Peter Coffin's inn that gave Ishmael shelter on a bitterly cold night.

CHAPTER 111: THE PACIFIC

The Pequod enters the Pacific Ocean, which Ishmael has always dreamed of seeing. He finds it mysterious, beautiful, and seductive, commenting on the coral reefs, the musk-scented breezes, and the lovers he imagines waking together in the woods of the various islands. Ahab, by contrast, is only aware that he is nearing his journey's end: Moby Dick is swimming somewhere in these waters.

CHAPTER 112: THE BLACKSMITH

Perth, the ship's blacksmith who forged the hardware for Ahab's new leg, is beset by demands from all the crew members; various weapons and objects need to be repaired or altered. He does all this work patiently and silently. Various crew members notice that he limps and they ask what happened to him. Perth explains that his feet were frostbitten years ago and have never fully recovered their feeling. This story leads to further questions and eventually he tells the crew his whole history.

On land, Perth was a happy and successful man with a young wife and three children. He ruined his life by succumbing to alcoholism; his business failed, he lost his house, and his wife and children died of hunger and neglect. Heartbroken and hopeless, Perth went to sea as his only alternative to suicide.

COMMENT

Note the parallel between Perth and Ahab. Both are disabled and walk with difficulty; both have young wives and children; both are fixed on a hopeless goal (Perth on the bottle, Ahab on his revenge). Perth brought disaster to his family, and Ahab may bring disaster to the crew, as Chapter 109 suggests.

CHAPTER 113: THE FORGE

About noon, as Perth is hammering away at a pike-head on his anvil, Ahab approaches the forge. Seeing the sparks flying all about the blacksmith, he asks how it is that Perth is never scorched; Perth replies that he is beyond scorching; he is scarred all over. Ahab asks if Perth can smooth out the pike-head so that it will be as good as new. Perth believes he can: he can smooth out all dents and seams except for one. Ahab seizes him by the shoulders, with a passionate outcry: Can Perth smooth out the seams and dents in Ahab's mind? These are the only wrinkles that Perth cannot remove. Ahab changes the subject, showing Perth a bag of nail-stubs from race-horses' shoes, and asks Perth to make him a harpoon.

COMMENT

This moment is almost an exact echo of a scene in Shakespeare's Macbeth. A doctor reports to Macbeth on the insane Lady Macbeth's condition. Macbeth asks sadly, "Cans't thou not minister to a mind diseas'd?" The doctor replies that the patient must cure herself of such ills, and Macbeth angrily returns to his preparations for war. Like Macbeth, Ahab has deliberately chosen a course which he knows will bring trouble and despair. Both men wish that they could have had peaceful and happy old ages, but both feel that they are condemned to the paths they follow.

Impressed with the quality of the nails, Perth forges them into twelve rods, which Ahab welds into one piece. Fedallah walks past and bows to the fire. After the shank is ready, Ahab gives Perth all his razors, ordering him to weld them onto the head for the point and barbs. Just as Perth is about to cool the whole thing in water, Ahab orders him to wait. He asks the three harpooneers to give him enough of their blood to temper the weapon, and they agree; Ahab then pours blood onto the scorching harpoon head with the words, "Ego non baptizo te in nomine patris, sed in nomine diaboli! (I baptize you not in the name of the Father, but of the devil!)" After this, he selects a strong hickory pole for the shaft, and weaving the line into the socket of the head, forces the pole firmly into place. The harpoon is complete. Ahab takes it to his cabin. The echo of Pip's pitiful laughter is heard.

COMMENT

This blasphemous parody of the Christian sacrament of baptism emphasizes the demoniacal nature of Ahab's quest. Note that the blood for tempering the blades is supplied by three of the non-Christian characters. Ahab's insistence on doing much of the work himself, with Perth helping him, emphasizes the deeply personal nature of his revenge.

CHAPTER 114: THE GILDER

The Pequod is now cruising in the heart of the Japanese whaling grounds, and the whaleboats are busy many hours every day. The weather is beautiful, the sea calm. Ishmael comments that it is easy to forget about the dangerous fish and animals below the sea's tranquil surface. The serenity of the atmosphere affects even Ahab: he feels comforted by it, but cannot forget that it will not last. Starbuck, gazing down from his boat into the water, recovers his faith; perhaps, after all, all will be well. Stubb is so delighted with his surroundings that he forgets that he has ever felt miserable.

COMMENT

The omniscient narrator allows us to look into the thoughts of Ahab, Starbuck, and Stubb as they contemplate the beauty of the Pacific. Each man's thoughts are consistent with his character. Ahab can take only a little comfort in such fleeting pleasure, Starbuck is restored to his deep faith, and Stubb is just having a good time.

The "gilder" of the chapter title is the sun: In the late afternoon, it lends a gold color to everything its light touches.

CHAPTER 115: THE PEQUOD MEETS THE BACHELOR

A few weeks later, the Pequod encounters the Bachelor, a Nantucket whale ship, which has filled its last oil cask and is on its way home. The Bachelor is decked out fantastically in celebration of her success: Pennants stream here and there; the mast-head men have streamers in their hats; a whale's jaw hangs under the bowsprit; a barrel of oil is hung high on each mast. The Bachelor's captain invites Ahab aboard for a gam, but Ahab only replies. "Hast seen the White Whale?" The captain replies cheerfully that he has heard of the white whale, but doesn't believe in him. He repeats his cordial invitation, but Ahab somberly refuses. As the two ships sail past one another, the Pequod's crew looks longingly after the Bachelor, but the Bachelor's happy crew has already forgotten the Pequod.

COMMENT

This is a chapter of contrasts. The Bachelor's officers and crew look cheerfully back at the recent past: The Pequod's officers and crew look apprehensively toward the near future. The Bachelor's captain is happy in his ignorance of Moby Dick: Ahab is grim in his knowledge.

CHAPTER 116: THE DYING WHALE

The next day, the Pequod captures four whales. One is killed by Ahab, very late in the day. Ahab notices that the whale turns his head toward the sunset as he dies (Ishmael tells us that all sperm whales do so), and murmurs to himself, "He too worships fire." As soon as the whale dies, the body slowly turns in the other direction.

COMMENT

Stubb has several times noticed Fedallah's worship of fire, and takes this as proof that Fedallah is a devil. Ahab also seems drawn to fire. Ahab is clearly not a devil, but a man who has turned his back on God.

CHAPTER 117: THE WHALE WATCH

The four whales killed by the Pequod are widely scattered; only three of them can be brought to the ship before dark. Ahab and his crew keep watch over the other. Ahab awakens to see Fedallah staring at him, and he tells the Parsee that he has dreamed of a hearse again. Fedallah makes three predictions. First he predicts that before Ahab dies he will see two hearses on the sea, one not made by mortal hands, and one made of American wood. Next, he predicts that he will go before Ahab to be his pilot: that is, that he will die first and lead Ahab into the next world. Third, he prophesies that only hemp can kill Ahab. Ahab laughs unpleasantly, he feels immortal at these words, because he is sure these circumstances will never occur.

COMMENT

Ahab takes Fedallah's reference to hemp as a threat of the gallows: rope is made of hemp, which implies death by hanging. A captain would never be hanged at sea unless his crew mutinied and were desperate enough to execute him. However, Ahab forgets that other items, such as whale-lines, are made of hemp.

This is almost the only time Fedallah has spoken in the novel, and the only time he and Ahab talk together. It is apparent that they have an understanding; Ahab has previously told Fedallah about his dreams, and Fedallah has made these predictions before.

CHAPTER 118: THE QUADRANT

On an especially brilliant and clear morning, Ahab comes on deck with his quadrant (a navigational instrument used to calculate a ship's precise position) and looks through it very carefully at the sun. Fedallah kneels on the deck behind him, bowing to the sun. Suddenly, Ahab curses the quadrant because it can only tell him where he is; it cannot tell him where he will be tomorrow, or where Moby Dick is. In a rage,

Ahab dashes the quadrant to the deck and crushes it, vowing to steer by compass and by log and line from now on. He does not notice the look of combined triumph and fatalistic despair on Fedallah's face at this gesture. Ahab roars out an order to change course. Starbuck asks Stubb what the result of such behavior can possibly be, and Stubb replies that he has overheard Ahab mutter that he must play the hand of cards that fate has dealt him.

COMMENT

The destruction of the quadrant underscores the fact that Ahab has no thought beyond chasing Moby Dick. The quadrant cannot help him track down his enemy, so it is useless to him. He gives no thought to the voyage home or the safety of the crew.

Once again, Ahab refers to himself as the tool of fate. He believes that he cannot control his own destiny; that he must chase Moby Dick, because this is his fate. Because he is a certain kind of person, he must act in a certain way; if he gave up the quest, he would no longer be Ahab.

MOBY-DICK
CHAPTERS 119–135

CHAPTER 119: THE CANDLES

That evening, a typhoon strikes the Pequod, tearing off several of her sails and rolling huge waves onto her deck. One wave smashes Ahab's whaleboat. Stubb makes a joke of the danger, and sings a rollicking song, but Starbuck warns him to be quiet; is Stubb unaware of the omens in the storm? The typhoon is from the east, the direction in which the Pequod sails in pursuit of Moby Dick, and Ahab's whaleboat has been crushed at exactly the spot where Ahab stands when hunting. Ahab's approach interrupts their conversation. Starbuck remembers the ship's lightning rods, and asks permission to lower them over the side for the ship's protection (they are on chains and can be hauled up after the storm has passed).

At this moment, the tops of the Pequod's three masts are lit up by corpusants (a light caused by atmospheric electricity, sometimes seen on mastheads, church towers, and other tall objects), and many of the crew are terrified by the eerie glow. Ahab shouts to attract the crew's attention, then seizes the lightning rod links and, with his foot upon the back of the kneeling Fedallah, says he is feeling the pulse of the lightning. Then he makes a defiant speech, asserting his unconquerable individuality in the face of the power of nature. Lightning flashes about the ship, and he speaks directly to it, calling it his ancestor and vowing his defiant worship of it. Suddenly the tip of his new harpoon, which is still in the smashed whaleboat, bursts into the same kind of flame that is playing over the mastheads. Starbuck shouts that this is a sign that God is against Ahab, and asks to be allowed to give orders to turn the ship toward home. Eager to obey Stabuck, the men spring to their posts, but Ahab picks up the fiery harpoon and says he will kill the first man who touches a rope. Horrified by Ahab, but even more by the flaming harpoon, the men scramble away from him.

COMMENT

In the middle of Ahab's speech to the lightning, Melville shifts narrative voices. He inserts a stage direction describing Ahab's pose against the flames surrounding the masts. Starbuck's cry of "Look at thy boat, old man!" literally interrupts Ahab's monologue and returns the chapter to the voice of the omnisceint narrator. This dramatic interjection has the effect of a close-up in a movie: it makes the reader a part of the crew, looking on the scene from the inside.

Ahab insists that nature has no power over him. It cannot change his character, and his character, his force of will, is what makes him pursue Moby Dick.

CHAPTER 120: THE DECK TOWARDS THE END OF THE FIRST NIGHT WATCH

As the storm continues, Starbuck addresses Ahab, who is standing by the helm. He wants permission to furl a sail, but Ahab refuses—he wants all left as it is. He merely orders that everything movable be lashed down. Only cowards take down sails, he says, or back down on their purposes, in bad weather.

CHAPTER 121: MIDNIGHT— THE FORECASTLE BULWARKS

Stubb and Flask argue as they lash down the anchors. Flask points out that Stubb has said that there were special dangers in sailing with Ahab, but Stubb replies that Ahab was in no more danger while holding the lightning rod links than any man would be standing near a mast on any ship in a storm. Stubb comments that he and Flask are lashing the anchors as tightly as if they will never use them again.

CHAPTER 122: MIDNIGHT ALOFT— THUNDER AND LIGHTNING

Tashtego is high on the mainmast, lashing down a sail. He imitates the rumble of the thunder, and wishes he had a glass of rum.

COMMENT

These three chapters continue the dramatic presentation begun in the Chapter 119. They open with stage
directions, and include dialogue with no commentary.

Starbuck continues to fail in his attempts to make Ahab
see reason. Ahab's will is stronger than Starbuck's. The
suspense mounts as the reader realizes more and more
clearly that Starbuck is right and Ahab is wrong: the
ship and the crew are in greater and greater danger, but
Ahab will not turn from his course.

Stubb continues to maintain his good humor in the face
of danger. Tashtego's reaction to the storm is pure
common sense: He would prefer rum to thunder. His
wish for rum, four lines of text, is the novel's shortest
chapter.

CHAPTER 123: THE MUSKET

Toward morning, the typhoon eases off enough so that
Starbuck and Stubbs can cut down the shreds of sail and
replace them with new canvas. The Pequod, buffeted about
in all directions during the storm, can pursue her eastward
course again. Starbuck goes below to report the change of
wind to Ahab, and pauses outside the cabin door next to the
weapons rack. He picks up the very musket with which Ahab
once threatened to kill him, and for agonizing moments
debates whether he should kill Ahab. Ahab's quest may well
cause the death of the entire crew—would Starbuck be guilty
of murder if he prevented Ahab from murdering the crew? He
considers taking Ahab prisoner instead, but realizes he would
not be able to stand the daily sight of Ahab's
despair and broken will. If he does anything, he will have to
kill him. Starbuck prays for advice, and then calls out to the
captain that the ship is on course again. Ahab cries loudly in
reply "Stern all! Oh, Moby Dick, I clutch thy heart at last!"
Starbuck realizes that Ahab has not heard him—that he has

shouted in his troubled sleep. He puts the musket back in the rack, returns to the deck, and sends Stubb to wake the captain and tell him the news.

COMMENT
Starbuck cannot bring himself to kill Ahab. Although he realizes that killing Ahab will ensure the safety of the ship and the crew, he cannot be sure that he is justified in God's eyes. It has been apparent in their scenes together that, besides any moral consideration, Starbuck feels deep pity and love for Ahab, and never would be able deliberately to murder him.

CHAPTER 124: THE NEEDLE
The following morning the Pequod is bowling along briskly on the waning winds of the storm. Ahab suddenly realizes that the sun is rising behind the ship; the Pequod is sailing west when he has set a course for the east! Ahab checks the compass, which reads east-south-east. He realizes that the storm has demagnetized the compass needles and reversed them exactly. Ahab gives orders to turn the ship about. Then, calling the crew together, he prepares another needle for the compass, acting with the air of a sorcerer (the process is a very simple one, but Ahab plays on the ignorance and superstition of the crew, as he has done before). The sailors are abashed and rather frightened at this evidence of Ahab's mysterious power.

COMMENT
This is the second time that a navigational device has been damaged: Ahab destroyed the quadrant, and the electrical force of the storm ruined the compass. The Pequod had turned its back on the quest and was headed for home until Ahab noticed the position of the sun. Ahab does not pay any attention to the warning: Although nature turned the ship out of its course, Ahab continues to try to master nature.

CHAPTER 125: THE LOG AND LINE

The Pequod's log and line, a device for measuring speed, has never been used on this voyage. But one morning, Ahab orders the log cast over the ship's stern. The old Manxman fears that the rope, rotted by salt spray and disuse, will break, but Ahab says it will hold. The log is heaved, and almost immediately the rope snaps. Ahab tells the seamen to mend the rope and have the carpenter make another log.

As the Manxman and his helper work to reel in the line, Pip gets in their way. He looks over the railing and asks if they are trying to haul the missing Pip aboard; they should leave him where he is. Cowards are not welcome on the Pequod. Ahab, touched by the sight of this pitiful madness, holds out his hand to Pip and tells him to make Ahab's cabin his home for the rest of the voyage. Pip takes his hand, immediately sensitive to Ahab's kindness. They promise never to let one another go, and leave the deck.

COMMENT

The log and line is another navigational device which has ceased to function properly.

Melville indicated in an earlier chapter that Pip has forgotten his identity: Pip remembers a boy named Pip who jumped out of the whaleboat, but he does not associate this missing boy with himself. It is apparent that the cause of his madness is a deep shame at his own terror.

In Chapter 113, Ahab told the blacksmith that he was "impatient of all misery in others that is not mad." Here he is confronted with both misery and madness, and his reaction is astonishingly gentle and kind. It is this kindness that makes Pip cling to him.

CHAPTER 126: THE LIFE-BUOY

One night just before dawn, as the ship is sailing into the equatorial cruising grounds, weird cries are heard near the Pequod. Ahab explains that seals looking for their young must have made the noises, but the crew nevertheless feels uneasy. Shortly after dawn, a sailor on mast-head watch falls with a cry into the sea, and, although the life-buoy is thrown overboard, he never rises to grasp it. The dried life-buoy itself, in fact, soaks up water and sinks. The sailors feel more relief than pity at the drowning of the seaman, for they feel that the omen of the terrible cries has now been fulfilled.

Starbuck searches the ship for a substitute for the life-buoy, but finds nothing suitable. Queequeg hints that his coffin would suffice. Starbuck orders the carpenter to seal the coffin tightly and hang it in the place of the buoy. The carpenter is annoyed at having to re-fit a piece of work he has already done, but obeys.

COMMENT

The first man to climb the mast to watch out for Moby Dick falls and drowns. Again, Ahab takes no warning.

The irony of a coffin being converted into a life-buoy is obvious. Note that when Queequeg first lay down in his coffin, he recovered almost immediately from an illness that everyone thought would kill him. His recovery suggests that the coffin may make a perfect life-buoy.

CHAPTER 127: THE DECK

The carpenter sets to work on the coffin. Ahab comes up on deck, calling back to Pip to wait in the cabin. He asks the carpenter what he is doing (the order to convert the coffin was given by Starbuck, not Ahab). The carpenter explains. Ahab accuses him of making legs one day and coffins the next—for interfering with both life and death. The carpenter is confused by this conversation, and Ahab leaves him alone, returning to Pip in the cabin.

COMMENT

Pip has kept his vow not to leave Ahab; he tries to follow him on deck.

The carpenter can make nothing of Ahab's questions about life and death. To him, the coffin is simply a wooden object designed for a particular purpose, and he now has orders to convert it to a different purpose.

Ahab finds the carpenter's practical attitude just as puzzling. Ahab cannot hear the carpenter's hammer knock on the coffin lid without recalling similar sounds in graveyards, and cannot hear an exclamation "Faith!" without asking "What is faith?" in the philosophical sense.

CHAPTER 128: THE PEQUOD MEETS THE RACHEL

The next day the Pequod sights the Rachel, a whaler from Nantucket. Her masts are full of lookouts, and as she sails up close to Ahab's ship, she cuts off the wind, causing the Pequod's sails to slacken with a clap. The Manxman mumbles, "she brings bad news." Ahab asks the Rachel's captain, Gardiner if he has seen the White Whale, and Gardiner replies, "Aye, yesterday. Have ye seen a whaleboat adrift?" Invited to board the Pequod, he explains that he has lost a boat, which was towed out of sight by Moby Dick. He asks the Pequod to get out its own boats to help in the search. Stubb, overhearing, assumes that one of the missing men must owe the captain money, since he is so anxious to recover the boat. Ahab's face is unresponsive, and Gardiner presses his request, explaining that his twelve-year-old son is among the missing. Stubb, ashamed of his cynicism, cries out that they must help search for the child. Gardiner reminds Ahab of his own son, and pleads for Ahab's understanding and help, but Ahab refuses. Now that he knows he is so near Moby Dick, he will not take the time needed to help in the search. Stunned, Gardiner returns to the Rachel, which continues her search alone.

COMMENT

Two things in particular heighten the horror of Ahab's refusal: his recent kindness to Pip, and Stubb's reaction to Gardiner's story. Because Ahab pitied Pip and treated him gently, the reader anticipates that he will willingly help Gardiner. His cruelty is all the more shocking because of the contrast.

Stubb's first reaction to the story—that two ships should not stop to look for a missing whaleboat at the height of the busy season—is typical of his character. Throughout the novel, Stubb has never been sensitive. His impulsive retraction on learning of the missing child, and his immediate readiness to help in the search, underline Ahab's callousness.

CHAPTER 129: THE CABIN

As Ahab starts out of his cabin to go up on deck, Pip takes his hand to go with him. Ahab tells him to stay behind, however, for he fears that his pity for Pip may sway him from his purpose. Pip promises devotion to Ahab; he will take the place of Ahab's lost leg, if Ahab will lean on him. Ahab still refuses to allow him on deck. He tries to reassure the boy by telling him to listen for the sound of his ivory stump pacing the deck; Pip will thus know that Ahab is nearby. The two clasp hands for a moment, and Ahab goes on deck. Left alone, Pip huddles in the cabin, afraid to move.

CHAPTER 130: THE HAT

Now that Ahab is so close to his goal, he can literally think of nothing else. His mood affects the officers and crew, all of whose humor vanishes. Ahab and Fedallah are always on deck; Ahab even eats his meals on the quarter-deck. Each dawn, Ahab calls out, "Man the mast-heads!" and the long watch begins, ending only well after sunset. After four days, however, Ahab suspects that no one but the three harpooners really wants to sight Moby Dick, so he rigs a special line and has himself raised to the main mast-head. Ironically, the man he chooses to see that his line remains secure is Starbuck—the one man of the entire crew who has openly opposed him and the one he would trust least to sing out if Moby Dick were sighted. Before Ahab is atop the mainmast ten minutes, a low-flying sea-hawk picks his hat off his head and flies off with it into the distance. Ishmael comments that this is a common occurrence at sea, but the Pequod's crew takes it as an omen.

COMMENT

In Chapter 72, Ishmael and Queequeg were linked together by a rope that meant life and death to them. Now Ahab and Starbuck are linked by a rope. The true friendship of Ishmael and Queequeg points up the very different relationship between the captain and the mate.

CHAPTER 131: THE PEQUOD MEETS THE DELIGHT

After a few more days of sailing, the Pequod meets the Delight, another Nantucket whaler. Ahab asks the Delight's captain, "Hast seen the White Whale?" The captain points to the remains of a smashed whaleboat hanging from the Delight's shears (beams running across the quarter-deck, the usual storage place for boats needing repair). "Hast killed him?" asks Ahab. The captain replies that no harpoon ever forged will kill Moby Dick. Triumphantly, Ahab holds up his own harpoon and cries out that he holds the needed weapon in his hand. The Delight's captain somberly responds that he has lost five men to Moby Dick: He is about to read the funeral service over the only one whose body was recovered. Ahab orders his crew to sail on, but the Pequod does not move out of range fast enough to avoid hearing the sound of the body as it splashes into the water. The Delight's crewmen see the coffin (the new life-buoy) hanging over the Pequod's stern as the ships sail apart.

COMMENT

The Delight is ironically named: it is the most somber of the ships the Pequod meets. It also conveys the sternest warning Ahab has yet received: that Moby Dick killed five men on the preceding day, and that he seems invulnerable to the weapons of a whaler. As always, Ahab ignores the warning.

CHAPTER 132: THE SYMPHONY

Ahab crosses the deck and leans over the Pequod's side. As he stares down into the sea, a tear falls into the water. Starbuck sees the captain, senses his unhappiness and wishes to comfort him, but hesitates to go too close or speak to Ahab. Ahab turns, sees Starbuck, and begins to speak, his resistance broken. He laments the solitude of command, the loneliness and fear of the young wife he has left behind, and the feelings of utter weariness and old age his useless quest has brought him. He asks Starbuck to remain on board the Pequod rather than taking out his boat, so that Starbuck will not run the risk Ahab will run of never seeing home and family again. Deeply moved by this appeal, Starbuck urges Ahab to change course and return to Nantucket. Together they remember beautiful summer mornings at home, and the faces of their wives and children. But Ahab cannot turn back now; he does not know whether he controls his quest, or whether it is his fate, but he must go on. Starbuck leaves his side in despair. Ahab slowly crosses to the other side of the deck, where he sees Fedallah leaning over the railing.

COMMENT

This scene between Starbuck and Ahab is one of the most emotional in the novel. The reader feels great sympathy and pity for both men. Starbuck is not strong enough to persuade Ahab to turn back to Nantucket, and Ahab is not strong enough to break the powerful grip that revenge has on him.

Note that Starbuck stands on one side of the deck and Fedallah on the other, and that Ahab crosses from Starbuck's side to Fedallah's side as he makes his decision to continue his pursuit of Moby Dick. Fedallah has been compared to the devil throughout the novel. Starbuck, by contrast, has many of the qualities of a minister of God.

CHAPTER 133: THE CHASE—FIRST DAY

That night, Ahab smells the unmistakable odor of a whale, and gives a slight change of course in the direction from which the smell seems to come. At daybreak the mast-heads are manned, and Ahab is the first to see the whale. It is Moby Dick at last. All the boats but Starbuck's are lowered, and the men paddle silently after the great whale. He swims swiftly, still unaware of the whaleboats chasing him. They have nearly caught up with him when suddenly he sounds. The boats wait, knowing he will have to resurface in an hour or less. Birds begin to circle near Ahab's boat (a sign that a whale is near), and, peering into the depths, Ahab sees Moby Dick's immense, open jaw rising toward him. The men whirl the boat around, but Moby Dick follows their move. As he surfaces, he grips the boat in the long scroll of his jaw, crunching it in half and dumping the crew into the sea. As Moby Dick swims off, Stubb's boat rescues Ahab and the others, and all return to the Pequod. Ahab asks after his harpoon; it is safe, and no men have been lost. Moby Dick is swimming so powerfully and strongly that the whaleboats cannot catch him; Ahab and the crew continue the chase in the Pequod. When night falls, the watch is given up until morning. Ahab announces to the crew that although he was the first one to see Moby Dick, he will leave the gold doubloon nailed to the mast. The first man to raise Moby Dick's corpse will win it, and if this is Ahab again, he will divide ten times the doubloon's worth among all the crew.

COMMENT

After hundreds of pages and more than a hundred chapters, the novel's title character finally appears on stage. Moby Dick is an impressive sight, for his size, strength, and unusual color. He lives up to his reputation for intelligence and apparent deliberate malice, employing strategy as well as force to destroy Ahab's boat. However, no blows are exchanged. Although Moby Dick could easily have killed Ahab and his crew, he is content with smashing their boat. They have no time to attack or wound him, and he does them no harm beyond the wrecked boat and a soaking in the ocean.

CHAPTER 134: THE CHASE—SECOND DAY

At dawn the mast-heads are manned again, and the Pequod continues the chase. The crew has forgotten its dread and forebodings in the excitement, and all are eager in pursuit. The watch mistakenly calls that he has seen Moby Dick early in the morning, but later, less than a mile ahead, the whale breaches—arcs his body fully into the air before he dives again.

Again the boats are lowered, and again Ahab tells Starbuck to stay with the ship. This time, however, Moby Dick charges the whaleboats instead of waiting to be attacked; he dashes among them with jaws open and tail lashing furiously. By skillful maneuvering the boats avoid him, and all three dart harpoons into his sides. As Moby Dick thrashes about in the sea, the lines become entangled and snarled all over his body. Although Ahab daringly cuts some of the lines with his knife, the tangle drags together the boats of Stubb and Flask, smashing them to bits. Moby Dick dips beneath the surface and rises again, capsizing Ahab's boat, then floats silently, feeling with his fins for objects in the water. Whenever he feels anything, he smashes down his monstrous tail. Then he swims placidly away as the Pequod sails up to rescue the boat crews. Ahab's ivory leg is snapped off in the battle.

Fedallah has been lost in the battle, as has Ahab's harpoon. Ahab is sure the harpoon is in the whale's side. He is apprehensive about Fedallah's death, remembering the harpooner's prophecy that he would die before Ahab and lead him to the next world. Undaunted, however, Ahab gives orders to continue on the whale's track. Starbuck cries out that Ahab must abandon his quest: The whole crew will be killed if he continues. Moby Dick cannot be harmed. Ahab can only answer "I am the Fate's lieutenant; I act under orders." During the night, the carpenter makes Ahab another new leg, and the Pequod follows Moby Dick.

CHAPTER 135: THE CHASE—THIRD DAY

The third morning is fair again, and the Pequod hastens onward. By noon, however, there is still no sign of the whale, and Ahab concludes that the ship has sailed past Moby Dick during the night ("He's chasing me now; not I him—that's bad"). The ship is turned about, and Ahab again has Starbuck hoist him up to the mast-head, where he sights Moby Dick after perhaps one hour's watch. Again three boats are lowered. Before Ahab leaves the ship, he calls Starbuck. The two bid one another an emotional farewell, shake hands, and Ahab gets into his boat. Starbuck remains with the ship. This time, however, a number of sharks follow Ahab's whaleboat.

In the distance Moby Dick dives, but the boats move onward slowly, hoping to be near him when he surfaces. Suddenly the sea around them swells, and Moby Dick races to the surface, his giant brow thirty feet in the air. Surging among the boats, he does enough damage to Stubb's and Flask's boats that they must go back to the ship for repairs. As Moby Dick turns, he exposes one of his flanks to Ahab. There on the whale's side, entangled in the snarled harpoon line, is the torn body of Fedallah. Ahab immediately recognizes the hearse "not made by mortal hands" that Fedallah prophesied in Chapter 117. Nonetheless Ahab races after the whale, and darts a harpoon into him. Moby Dick knocks one oarsman completely out of the boat; this man is left floating astern. The whale snaps the line, and turns upon his pursuers—but instead of attacking Ahab, he charges the Pequod, which he sees bearing down on the scene. Ahab tries desperately to head him off, but he cannot; Moby Dick's immense forehead staves in the Pequod's starboard bow, and the ship rapidly fills with water. Ahab, enraged, darts another harpoon into Moby Dick, but as he stoops to clear a snarl in the line, it loops around his neck and snaps him out of the boat in an instant. The ship sinks with all hands. The whirlpool created by the battle settles, and "the great shroud of the sea rolled on as it rolled five thousand years ago."

COMMENT

Fedallah's prophecies are fulfilled. He dies before Ahab; the two hearses are Moby Dick (not made by mortal hands) and the Pequod (made of American wood), and the hemp that drags Ahab to his death is the whale line.

The novel contains only one clue that Moby Dick survives this encounter. This clue is in Chapter 54, the only section of the novel that takes place after the Pequod's journey. When Ishmael repeats the tale of Radney and Steelkilt, he refers to Moby Dick as "immortal."

EPILOGUE

In a brief epilogue, Ishmael explains that he was the only survivor of the Pequod's encounter with Moby Dick. He was in Ahab's boat, and was thrown clear of the conflict during the third day of the chase. He was able to remain afloat, and watched Ahab's death and the ship's wreck. The coffin/life-buoy shoots to the surface of the water, and Ishmael swims to it and holds on. Two days later, he is rescued by the Rachel, still searching for her captain's son.

COMMENT

Note that a coffin, of all things, saves Ishmael's life. It is significant that the coffin belonged to Queequeg, Ishmael's closest friend. It is also significant that the inn kept by a man named Coffin first gave Ishmael shelter at the beginning of the novel, and that Queequeg recovered from his apparently fatal illness after his coffin was first made and he lay down in it.

The Epilogue is the only chapter in the novel that opens with an epigraph—a brief quotation at the start of a chapter that relates to the chapter's themes or plot. The epigraph is a line from the book of Job. It is a refrain, the final words of each of four messengers who bring the hitherto happy and prosperous Job the devastating news that his livestock, his shepherds and cowherds, and his sons have all been killed. These disasters are tests from God, but Job does not know that.

CHARACTER ANALYSES

AHAB

Ahab is a tragic hero; an admirable, larger-than-life man who brings about his own destruction because of a tragic flaw. Ahab recognizes his flaw, but feels powerless to correct it. He believes that if he did change course, he would cease to be Ahab: He must act according to his nature, no matter what the consequences.

Before Ahab lost his leg to Moby Dick, he was known as a good man. His nature was always solemn, but he was respected as a commander. He was well-educated, well-traveled, experienced in his profession, and always commanded respect. Peleg, who sailed with him as mate, describes him as "a grand, ungodly, god-like man." Starbuck addresses him several times as "noble heart." It is no accident that Ahab is named for a king. He also succeeded in winning the love and the hand in marriage of a much younger woman, and fathered a child. However, since the accident, his personality has changed. He has become what the reader sees in the novel: moody, savage, and intent on revenge.

Ahab pursues his revenge in spite of his recognition that it is bound to end in disaster. Throughout the novel, as Starbuck again and again objects to his plans or urges him to give up the chase, he admits that Starbuck is right and that he wishes he could give in. However, he considers himself the tool of—perhaps fate, perhaps God. "Is Ahab, Ahab?" he asks Starbuck. "Is it I, God, or whom, that lifts this arm?" It is his nature to act as he acts: he must pursue this revenge because he is Ahab, and this is what Ahab is like. Ahab's nature is defiant, so he must act defiant.

Ahab is an active man, but he is also thoughtful. He meditates on the meaning of everything he sees, although he frequently reaches the same conclusions about death and gloom. He looks beneath the surface of all the situations he is in throughout the novel.

MOBY DICK

Moby Dick is the novel's title character, and he is the motivating force behind all the action. Everything Ahab does in the novel, he does in pursuit of Moby Dick; the Pequod's entire crew is caught up in the same chase. Although he does not appear in the story until its final three chapters, he is the focus of all the attention throughout. Ishmael's many chapters on whales in general apply to Moby Dick in particular; through these chapters, the reader is given a detailed biography of the whale.

Moby Dick stands out among sperm whales for his exceptional size, strength, and intelligence. He has survived many battles with whalemen and harpooners, and has killed many of them. On one occasion, he destroyed an evil man, Radney of the whaler Town-Ho.

Many characters in the novel take Moby Dick at face value; his is a big, strong whale, crafty and cunning because of all his experience fighting whalers for his life, and apparently impossible to subdue—but incapable of malice, because he is only an animal who does not understand human language or feel human emotions.

The events of the novel, however, suggest that Moby Dick is more than just a strong and smart whale; he has a symbolic significance which goes beyond this. He symbolizes the unconquerable; the sea, nature, fate, the wrath of God. It is significant that Moby Dick survives the final meeting with Ahab and the Pequod.

ISHMAEL

Ishmael talks to the reader throughout the novel. However, once the Pequod sails, he fades into the background. He has no further conversation with any character; his function is simply to report on the voyage. Because Ishmael is new to whaling and has met none of the officers or crew but Queequeg before, he is the ideal detatched narrator. Since he is on the scene, he can describe events reliably and can talk knowledgeably about whaling. However, he has no role in Ahab's internal conflict, nor any relationship with the ship's officers.

Ishmael serves as Melville's mouthpiece to discuss whales and whaling as a metaphor for all life. Ishmael has given a great deal of thought to this in the time between the Pequod's voyage and publishing his account of it, and he has also done a great deal of research into whaling. It is not entirely clear what Ishmael has done since the Pequod's voyage, other than writing it down, but he mentions a gam aboard the Enderby and an evening with Spanish friends in Lima who are not whalers (they have never heard of Moby Dick).

STARBUCK
Starbuck functions as Ahab's good angel, but unfortunately he is not sufficiently strong to sway the captain. He is a truly good man, compassionate toward his misguided leader, and constantly aware of his responsibilities as first officer. Starbuck realizes both the physical and moral dangers of Ahab's quest, and does everything in his power to make him turn back. Starbuck is a conscientious man and constantly worried about the welfare of everyone around him. He risks open disagreement with Ahab on a number of occasions. Although he is well aware of his duty to obey his superior officer, he is more concerned with his duty to the ship and her crew.

STUBB
Unlike the cerebral Ahab and the emotional Starbuck, Stubb is a practical and cheerful man who is not given to thought. When he confronts physical danger, he does not run, but tries to keep his courage up by singing and joking. He is completely insensitive: It never occurs to hm that Pip will lose

his mind from the fear of being abandoned in the ocean. He observes Ahab's strange moods, but shrugs at them, deciding they are not his business. He is the perfect embodiment of the man who does not want to get involved; the man whose detatchment can be in part responsible for many disasters.

QUEEQUEG

Queequeg is a friendly, loyal, and intelligent man. He left his own land to travel and educate himself among Christians, but quickly realized that many Christians were hypocrites. However, he remained among them in order to help them as best he could. At least twice during the novel, Queequeg risks his own life to save someons else's, and it is his coffin that sustains Ishmael in the water until the Rachel comes to rescue him. Queequeg embodies the true morality of a good heart.

PIP

Pip's two main qualities are fear and devotion. Early in the book, during a storm, he was frightened by the noise and lightning, and he is so terrified by the whales that he leaps from the boat in an attempt to escape them. Unable to face his fears and master them, he forgets his own identity, speaking of Pip as if Pip were another person, a missing boy who fell overboard. When Ahab speaks kindly to him, Pip responds with love and gratitude. His promise never to desert the captain nearly melts Ahab's heart, but is not sufficient to make him turn back.

FEDALLAH (a.k.a. "The Parsee")

Fedallah is Ahab's bad angel, as Starbuck is his good angel. These roles are most strongly represented in Chapter 132, when Starbuck and Fedallah stand on opposite sides of the deck and Ahab crosses from Starbuck's side to Fedallah's after rejecting Starbuck's plea to turn the ship back toward Nantucket.

Fedallah is more a symbol than a character, and he is an ambiguous symbol at that. He speaks very little in the novel, and has no relationship with any character but Ahab. Stubb immediately identifies Fedallah as a devil, and never alters his opinion. Melville supports this interpretation with a number of images of Fedallah worshipping fire. However, Fedallah seems to reflect the evil in Ahab's nature rather than to affect it. Melville deliberately leaves this relationship unclear: Ahab and Fedallah have only one brief conversation in the novel (Chapter 117), and although Fedallah predicts several things that come to pass in the final three chapters, Melville never implies that Fedallah has any direct role in bringing them about.

PERTH

The blacksmith serves mainly as a warning to Ahab. His story parallels Ahab's almost exactly. Both men are unable to walk properly (one has an ivory leg, one limps from an old frostbite injury). Both men married much younger women and fathered children. Both men were happy in their marriages and successful in their professions. Ahab is obsessed with Moby Dick, and Perth was obsessed with alcohol. As a result of his obsession, Perth's life has been ruined and he has become a quiet, broken shell of himself.

CRITICAL COMMENTARY

Moby-Dick was published in London in mid-October, 1851, under the title *The Whale;* in New York, on November 14, it was published as *Moby-Dick, or The Whale.* Several reviews were printed in England in late October and early November. The attitude of the critics was varied, but the general tone of the reviews was negative. Two very influential periodicals, the *Athenaeum* and the *Spectator,* treated the book harshly. Even the favorable reviews tended to question the book's form or style, and many were disturbed by Melville's attitude toward organized religion.

In November, the first American reviews of *Moby-Dick* were printed. Generally they were quite favorable, perhaps partly because Melville's earlier works, *Typee* and *Omoo,* had been very popular. But as time passed, reviews of the book became less and less favorable; in a few years the book was all but forgotten. When Melville died in 1891, he was remembered not for *Moby-Dick,* but for *Typee* and *Omoo.*

The story of the revival of Melville's reputation is one of the most interesting in the history of American literature. It may be said to have begun in 1921 with a biography by Raymond Weaver, called *Herman Melville, Mariner and Mystic.* Weaver called *Moby-Dick* "indisputably the greatest whaling novel." In 1929 came another key book, Lewis Mumford's *Herman Melville.* Mumford's book is an attempt to understand the workings of Melville's mind rather than the facts of his life. His book is a daring and speculative one, which uses Melville's fiction, to a certain extent, as autobiographical documents. This attempt to integrate Melville's life and his works inspired further studies. Investigations of various kinds—some speculative, some of a most rigidly factual nature—followed for the next ten years.

In 1939, Charles R. Anderson published an important study of

Melville's three years in the South Pacific. It shows that Melville shaped and transformed factual material rather than simply inventing fantastic adventures.

From the mid-1940s to the mid-1950s, many books on Melville were published. W. E. Sedgwick, in *Herman Melville: The Tragedy of Mind* (1945), finds a trinity in *Moby-Dick*. Ahab, representing man, comes into conflict with Moby Dick, representing "the immense mystery of creation." The third element of this trinity is the ocean, which represents "truth." In 1949 appeared Richard Chase's *Herman Melville: A Critical Study*, a book with a very strong psychological and symbolic bias. Chase felt that the most important theme of Melville's work before *Moby-Dick* was that of the young man's awakening, or introduction to experience (a common theme in romantic literature). Chase's book asserts a good deal that it makes no attempt to prove. One year later, Newton Arvin published a short, highly readable biography called simply *Herman Melville*. The best chapter in the book is called "The Whale." Among other things, Arvin suggests that the form of *Moby-Dick* is closer to heroic poetry and the epic than to any other literary type. He discusses the structure, symbolism, and language of the book effectively. But many readers and critics find his treatment of Moby Dick as a symbol of "the father" an objectionable one. Arvin stresses the sexual innuendoes found in the novel, as does Leslie Fiedler in a more recent work, *Love and Death in the American Novel* (1960). The relationship of Ishmael and Queequeg, for instance, and the descriptions of the whale, are anatomized at length by these two writers and by others who have found the Freudian approach to Melville fruitful.

In a sense, the next biographical study counteracts many of the views of both Chase and Arvin. Leon Howard, in *Herman Melville* (1950), rejects the critical concept that assumes the subconscious mind to be of primary importance in writing. "In dealing with Melville's books," Howard wrote, "I have concerned myself primarily with the observable evidence of their growth." In 1951, a fresh look at Melville was provided by an Englishman, Ronald Mason, in a book called *The Spirit Above the Dust: A Study of Herman Melville*. Mason admits that there are some "loose ends" in "a book which by its very compendiousness could hardly hope to avoid them," but feels that *Moby-Dick* is nevertheless a great work; the transformation of "symbolic images into a creative myth, embodying a significant reflection of the profoundest human preoccupations, was Melville's achievement in *Moby-Dick*." For Mason, *Moby-Dick* embodies Melville's own philosophic despair: "the finest novel America has yet given to the world, it proclaims unmistakably Melville's spiritual desolation."

Crtiticism and commentary on Melville and *Moby-Dick* has continued to mount in the last decade, especially in articles and essays. A vast range of attitudes toward the book has been expressed: It has been read as myth, poem, political allegory, psychological document, and in various other ways.

ESSAY QUESTIONS AND ANSWERS

QUESTION

Moby-Dick is often considered an epic. In what ways does the work fit the category of epic?

ANSWER

An epic is a long narrative that presents characters of high position in a series of adventures of high significance. Usually the epic is unified around a central figure of heroic stature, and generally it deals with actions of great importance to a nation or people. Moby Dick is clearly a long tale of adventures that are profoundly meaningful, for they make us feel deeply the dangers of pride and hatred, and they bring forth much of the inexplicable mystery of life. Ahab is a character of gigantic proportions, even though we may shudder at him even as we admire (and perhaps pity) him. Symbolically, the actions are important on a national level, for the story can be read as an allegory of the risks involved in trying to subjugate nature to the will of man.

Besides these general considerations, *Moby-Dick* is epic in several specific ways. It describes a long journey. It includes a number of battles. Omens and the intervention of the deity function significantly in the novel as in the epic. The extensive description of the implements of whaling and the ways of a whaler's life parallel the description of arms and warriors in early epics.

QUESTION

What is the effect of Melville's variety of narrative techniques?

ANSWER

Most of the novel is narrated in the first person by Ishmael. Because Ishmael has no personal relationship with any character except Queequeg, and no special personal stake in the Pequod's voyage, he presents the characters and events objectively. He has opinions, but he is basically detatched from the conflicts of the story.

Melville occasionally uses a dramatic method, writing as though Moby Dick were a play, complete with stage directions. Melville uses this method to present soliloquies as well as conversations. This method allows the reader to experience scenes directly, unfiltered through any narrative point of view. The soliloquies give the reader windows into various characters' thoughts.

Occasionally, Melville makes use of an omniscient third-person narrator. This narrator can report conversations at which Ishmael could not have been present, such as the conversation between Starbuck and Stubb about Fedallah in Chapter 73.

QUESTION
Why does Melville include so much factual detail about whales and whaling?

ANSWER
Ishmael's running commentary on whales and whaling accomplishes two things. It provides a detailed biography of the title character, who is not directly introduced to the reader until the book is nearly over, and it allows Melville to speculate on a number of philosophical questions.

Moby Dick is the title character of the novel. Because he provides the motivation for the novel's human characters, he is in many ways its central focus. In many respects, he is the most important character. However, in choosing to write a realistic novel about an animal who cannot talk, and who must, because of the plot, remain offstage until the final thirty pages, Melville was faced with a problem. His solution is unique. Through the descriptions of whales and whaling, Melville provides the reader with a running biography of his title character. Almost in the manner of a detective story, the whaling chapters build up a more and more detailed portrait of the unseen object of the quest—a portrait that is finally completed with Moby Dick's appearance in Chapter 133.

The whaling chapters also provide the raw material out of which Ishmael can develop the meaning of Ahab's quest and of his own experience. The whale is Melville's metaphor for the whole of experience: It is alive and changing, complex and impossible to explain, mysterious and beautiful, and powerful and terrifying. All these aspects are underscored as, from time to time, Ishmael ponders one or another part or characteristic of the whale.

BIBLIOGRAPHY

There are many books and hundreds of articles on Melville and *Moby-Dick*. A selection of these is listed below.

Beginning with *Typee* in 1968, Northwestern University and the Newberry Library have been publishing definitive editions of Melville's complete works. Several volumes, correspondence as well as novels, are now available.

Auden, W.H. *The Enchaféd Flood, or The Romantic Iconography of the Sea.* University of Virginia Press (1950). In his discussion of the sea in Western literature and the nature of the Romantic hero, Auden provides a thorough, concise analysis of several aspects of *Moby-Dick.*

Barbour, James, and Tom Quirk, eds. *Writing the American Classics.* University of North Carolina Press (1990). Includes an essay by Barbour titled "'All My Books Are Botches': Melville's Struggle with *The Whale.*"

Bloom, Harold, ed. *Herman Melville.* Chelsea House Publishers (1986). A volume of essays in the Modern Critical Views series.

Bloom, Harold, ed. *Herman Melville's Moby Dick.* Chelsea House Publishers (1986). A volume of essays in the Modern Critical Interpretations series.

Boswell, Jeanetta. *Herman Melville and the Critics: A Checklist of Criticism 1900–1978.* Scarecrow Press (1981).

Bowen, Merlin. *The Long Encounter: Self and Experience in the Writings of Herman Melville.* University of Chicago Press (1960). Develops the interesting idea that Melville's characters fall into three basic types: those who fight fate, those who give in, and those who preserve "armed neutrality." Helpful short chapter introduction.

Braswell, William. *Melville's Religious Thought*. Octagon Books (1943). Now somewhat dated, but still the most complete introduction to this aspect of Melville.

Bryant, John, ed. *A Companion to Melville Studies*. Greenwood Press (1986).

Cameron, Sharon. *The Corporeal Self: Allegories of the Body in Melville and Hawthorne*. Columbia University Press (1981).

Chase, Richard. *Herman Melville: A Critical Study*. Hafner Publishing Company (1949). A controversial, but stimulating book that stresses mythic and psychological aspects of Melville's fiction. Tries to see Melville both as artist and in relation to cultural problems.

Chase, Richard. *The American Novel and Its Tradition* Johns Hopkins (1957). Considers *Moby-Dick* as an "epic romance." Many stimulating comments in a few pages.

Chase, Richard, ed. *Melville: A Collection of Critical Essays* (1962). Includes some of the essays printed in the Stern collection but broader in scope.

Dimock, Wai-Chee. *Empire for Liberty: Melville and the Poetics of Individualism*. Princeton University Press (1989).

Feidelson, Charles Jr. *Symbolism in American Literature*. University of Chicago Press (1953). Sees *Moby-Dick* as the high point of a symbolic movement in nineteenth-century American literature.

Frank, Stuart M. *Herman Melville's Picture Gallery Sources and Types of the "Pictorial" Chapters of Moby Dick*. E. J. Lefkowicz (1986).

Freeman, John. *Herman Melville*. Haskell (1974). Part of the American Literature series.

Gilmore, Michael T., ed. *Twentieth-Century Interpretations of Moby Dick*. Prentice Hall (1977).

Higgins, Brian. *Herman Melville: A Reference Guide*. G. K. Hall (1987).

Higgins, Brian. *Herman Melville: An Annotated Bibliography*. G. K. Hall (1979).

Hillway, Tyrus, and Luther Mansfield, eds. *Moby-Dick Centennial Essays*. Southern Methodist University Press (1953). Contains several excellent short pieces.

Howard, Leon, *Herman Melville: A Biography*. University of California Press (1951). The most trustworthy biography for the facts of Melville's life.

Irey, Eugene F, ed. *Moby-Dick Index/Concordance*. Hendricks House (1978).

Karcher, Carolyn. *Shadow over the Promised Land: Slavery, Race, and Violence in Melville's America*. Louisiana State University Press (1980).

Lawrence, D. H. *Studies in Classic American Literature*. Viking Penguin (1923, 1951). Devotes two very provocative chapters to Melville. Brilliant, but dangerous.

Levin, Harry. *The Power of Blackness*. Ohio University Press (1958). Treats Poe, Hawthorne, and Melville as writers who focus on the dark side of human nature.

Lewis, R. W. B. *The American Adam* (1957). Discusses the theme of the American as a "new man." One chapter on Melville.

Leyda, Jay. *The Melville Log*. Gordian (1951). A compendium of data about Melville, arranged chronologically (in two volumes). Leyda lets the reader make his own judgments about what the facts mean for Melville's life.

Markels, Julian. *Melville and the Politics of Identity*. University of Illinois Press (1993).

Martin, Robert K. *Hero, Captain, Stranger*. University of North Carolina Press (1986).

Mason, Ronald. *The Spirit Above the Dust, a Study of Herman Melville*. Appel (1951). Gives a fresh view in many ways, because the author is English. Central theme is that Melville concentrates on innocence in his early works, the loss of innocence later, and the triumph of innocence in *Billy Budd,* Melville's posthumous story.

Matthiessen, F. O. *American Renaissance*. Oxford University Press (1940). A brilliant discussion of five authors, including Melville. Especially good for social significance of Melville; excellent discussions of language.

McSweeney, Kerry. *Moby Dick: Ishmael's Mighty Book* (1986).

Morrison, Toni. "Unspeakable Things Unspoken: The Afro-American Presence in American Literature." *Michigan Quarterly Review* 28 (Winter, 1989).

Mumford. Lewis. *Herman Melville*. Harcourt Brace (1929). Develops a picture of Melville as a daring imaginative giant.

Olsen, Charles. *Call Me Ishmael*. Johns Hopkins University Press (1947). An exciting, if opinionated, book. Especially good for the influence of Shakespeare upon *Moby-Dick* and for the importance of space to Melville. Suggests that the Pequod symbolizes American industry and Ahab the American who is trying to subdue physical nature.

Parker, Hershel. *Herman Melville: A Biography, Volume I, 1819–1851*. Johns Hopkins University Press (1996).

Parker, Hershel, and Harrison Hayford, eds. *Moby-Dick as Doubloon: Essays and Extracts*. Norton (1970).

Percival, M. O. *A Reading of Moby Dick*. Hippocrene Books (1950). A good general guide and introduction to the novel— a running commentary.

Reynolds, David S. *Beneath the American Renaissance: The Subversive Imagination in the Age of Emerson and Melville*. Alfred A. Knopf (1989). Excellent analysis and discussion of thematic and cultural elements in the works of major American nineteenth-century writers, including Melville.

Rosenberry, Edward. *Melville and the Comic Spirit*. Harvard University Press (1955). As the title implies, this work takes up the "other side" of Melville.

Sedgwick, W. E. *Herman Melville, the Tragedy of Mind*. Russell & Russell (1945). Concentrates on the development of Melville's "inner vision" rather than dealing with the works specifically as literature.

Smith, Henry Nash. *Democracy and the Novel*. Oxford University Press (1978). Includes an essay titled "The Madness of Ahab."

Stern, Milton, ed. *Discussions of Moby-Dick* Heath. Heath (1960). An outstanding collection of essays, covering several major points and representing a number of critical viewpoints. Especially helpful for the "gams."

Stovall, Floyd, ed. *Eight American Authors*. Norton (1956). This book discusses the contents of the works it lists, and is extremely helpful as a general orientation for criticism of Melville.

Ujhazy, Maria. *Herman Melville's World of Whaling.* State Mutual Books (1982).

Vincent, Howard P. *The Trying-Out of Moby Dick.* Kent State University Press (1949). A study of the materials Melville used to write the novel. Demonstrates the importance of the whaling material to the book's theme.

Welles, Orson. *Moby Dick—Rehearsed. A Drama in Two Acts.* Samuel French, Inc. (1965). Welles' dramatization of *Moby-Dick* is as original and fascinating as all his other work. In his play, a number of actors meet to rehearse a blank-verse adaptation of Melville's novel.

Wright, Nathalia. *Melville's Use of the Bible.* Duke University Press (1949). Traces Melville's use of the language, characters, images, and themes of the Bible.

NOTES